AWAKENING

Life Lessons from the Sidhe

AWAKENING

Life Lessons from the Sidhe

Rionagh na Ard

RavenSidhe Publishing
Meridian, Idaho

Copyright © 2014 Rionagh na Ard

All rights reserved. This book may neither be stored in any information storage and retrieval system, nor transmitted or reproduced in whole or in part by any means, whether electronic, mechanical, photocopying, recording, or other, without the written consent of the publisher. Brief passages may be quoted in reviews.

The contents of this book are offered as opinion and personal experience only; author/publisher is not liable for anything that may result from reading or following the practices contained herein.

Published by RavenSidhe Publishing, LLC
Meridian, ID
www.ravensidhe.com

Publisher's Cataloging-in-Publication Data
na Ard, Rionagh.
   Awakening : life lessons from the Sidhe / Rionagh na Ard.
   p. cm.
   ISBN 978-0-9912113-3-3

1. Fairies. 2. Channeling (Spiritualism). 3. Celts—Religion. 4. Mythology, Celtic. 5. Wisdom—Religious aspects. 6. Conduct of Life. 7. Guides (Spiritualism). 8. Spiritual life. 9. Self-actualization (Psychology)—Religious aspects. I. Title.
BF1301 N22 2014
133.93 —dc23   2014941440

First Printing June 2014
10 9 8 7 6 5 4 3 2 1
Printed in the United States of America
Set in Alegreya and Alegreya Sans. Titles set in Eterna.
Library of Congress Control Number : 2014941440

This book is dedicated to the Sidhe, and to my Sidhe and human families.

ACKNOWLEDGMENTS

A number of beings on both sides of the veil have my gratitude regarding many things, including the creation of this book. Among them are the Morrigan, Niall na Ard, Faustina Peters, Val Roberts, Slieb Greeley, Nancy Parker, Rua Brithem, and Blu Womyn.

CONTENTS

Preface.....1

Introduction.....3

Chapter One: Sidhe Connections.....7

Chapter Two: Energy Work.....41

Chapter Three: Healing.....63

Chapter Four: Life Lessons.....85

Chapter Five: Everyday Magic.....129

Chapter Six: Human and Sidhe Relationships.....155

Chapter Seven: Life and the Afterlife.....169

Chapter Eight: Reflections on Consciousness.....187

Chapter Nine: Awakening.....199

Afterward.....211

*Take me with you
To your mountains, your glens, your meadows,
Beneath your sun, your moon, your stars.
Keep me close at your side and deep in your heart,
That I may hear your laughter on the wind
Across the veil and beyond.*

PREFACE

When I first began compiling this work in 2009, I thought it was to be a combination of helpful channeled writings that I had obtained from my Sidhe spirit guide, interspersed with journal entries and anecdotes of my personal journey while working with him. In large part, that is still the case. But then one day in the spring of 2010 I went to read Tarot at a healing fair, and nothing has been the same since. In the process of trading readings with others, I received some information that clarified my understanding of myself and cast a bright light upon my path. It confirmed something that many other readers, psychic intuitives and very perceptive friends had been telling me for years, but which I had never before allowed myself to believe.

The question I finally found the courage to ask was whether I was actually one of the Sidhe, currently incarnated in a human body. I'd put off asking this question for a very long time, mostly because I was not quite ready to know the answer, and I didn't want to be presumptuous. When the answer that came from my spirit guides via another reader turned out to be "yes," it was all I could do not to cry right there in public, because it made sense of so many random events and readings over the years, not to mention flashes of memory that did not fit with my current human life.

That same night, I had a further bit of synchronous confirmation from an unexpected source, followed over the next few years by many other confirmations, signs and events too specific to be mere coincidence, showing me that the time for doubt was past. Finally, I had the truth for which my soul had been searching for far longer than just the space of a single human lifetime.

Aside from anecdotes from my "Awakening," this book contains a great many pieces of advice given to me directly via mental communication with the Sidhe over the past few years, all of which brought me a great deal of comfort, a greater understanding and perception, a deeper connection to Spirit, and some profound inner healing.

It is my hope that in sharing this material, I may be able to help someone else on their own path of Spirit, whatever that path may be—human, Sidhe, or something else entirely. As with any and all information, however, you should take whatever is useful to you and disregard the rest, trusting in your own inner Knowing to find what resonates for you.

Blessings,
Rionagh na Ard
June 2012

INTRODUCTION

While some people feel particularly connected to the small plant devas and little winged pixies depicted in stories and folklore, these are not the beings I'm talking about in this book. The Sidhe to whom I refer are the tall, wise, ethereal beings most often spoken of in Celtic myth and legend—the Tuatha De Danann of Irish mythology, as well as related groups in other countries. However, regardless of these initial associations, the beings who nowadays are often collectively referred to as Sidhe are not necessarily confined to any particular geographic location.

Most countries have references in their folklore to Otherworldly beings with similar characteristics. Over the centuries, they have been known by many names and encountered under many guises. Though belief in their existence has waxed and waned during the course of human history, many of the Sidhe are nonetheless ready and willing to work with humans to correct imbalances in nature and foster a better understanding between our peoples that would have lasting benefits for both.

Quite a few books have been published detailing others' experiences with faery folk and the practice of what is sometimes referred to as the faery faith. This book is not intended to reinvent the wheel in that department, or to clone material already out there. In fact, until I realized how much information I was receiving from my Sidhe contacts, I wasn't sure it was going to be a book at all. Consequently, much of the information was directed to me personally, as the tone of the communications will often reflect.

What follows in the first chapter is a bit of background on me and how I discovered my connection to the Sidhe. The subsequent chapters get into the nuts and bolts of what it's like for me to hear and interact with them on a daily basis. Included are dated journal entries and accounts of lucid dreams or out-of-body experiences I've had with them.

Most of the chapters contain information I channeled from my Sidhe guide and husband as he began to teach me how to change my current human life for the better. Rather than giving me a dry tome full of primarily esoteric new-agey information, he has included a great deal of simple, practical advice for everyday life as well as a few tidbits pertaining to the Sidhe themselves. Topics range from insight on anger, guilt, stress and other typical daily frustrations, to physical health, energy work, relationships, and the afterlife.

This interaction has transformed my life and set me on a far different path than I'd ever imagined—a journey back to my soul's true home. Aside from the physical health benefits I've experienced, I have never felt such a deep sense of peace, even in the middle of the current stressful global economic and political climates.

INTRODUCTION

Given my genetic heritage and my longtime interest in Celtic culture, myths and legends, it makes perfect sense to me that on my quest to discover the roots of my personal spirituality, I came into contact with beings from the Celtic pantheon. But what I discovered in meeting and working with the Sidhe was something that went far beyond more conventional ideas about interactions with faeries or Celtic deities. There was no roadmap for the path I found myself taking.

Even in my dealings with particular Sidhe who many people consider to be deities, I did not find what I would perceive as gods or goddesses when I made contact with them, and they never indicated that they expected me to treat them as such. They are powerful entities, yes. But what they have truly been to me during this whole process is guides, mentors, teachers, healers, and in certain cases, longtime friends and beloved family.

Those Sidhe with whom I ended up working the most closely already had personal knowledge of and relationships with me, whether I remembered it at first or not, and so my initial connections with them were more in the nature of reconnections, re-establishing working relationships that were already in place long before I incarnated into my current human lifetime. I found myself walking into the interactions without fear, and with a distinct feeling of coming home.

AWAKENING

CHAPTER ONE

SIDHE CONNECTIONS

I was lucky enough to grow up with a forest for a backyard. It was my solace, my place of refuge when life was difficult. I felt constantly drawn to it, and spent a lot of time under its lush green canopy of pine and fir. My childhood swing set was positioned in the forest's edge, where the trees provided just the right amount of shade in the summer, without being so far removed that I could not see the house from where I was.

There was a large moss-covered outcropping not far behind the swings, and often as I played, I had the distinct sensation that someone was watching me from the rock. I often found myself looking over my shoulder to see whether anyone was there, even though I believed myself to be alone.

Sometimes, greatly daring, I ventured quite close to the outcropping, which had several notable cracks running through it. Occasionally, I imagined that someone or something would come out of the crack in the stone to get me and take me away somewhere inside, perhaps to another world. I had no explanation for why I had this notion, and no such event ever occurred, but I was never able to shake the feeling of being watched whenever I was near the stone.

Many years later, I returned to that forest fully aware of whom and what I was, and looked again on the rock outcropping that had held so much fascination for me as a child. I took several photos that day as a remembrance, including the one on the cover of this book, which turned out to be distinctly different from all of the others. In it, you see the shining orb-form of my Sidhe beloved, as well as another larger but less distinct orb, which I understand to be the guardian spirit who resides there.

Their appearance in the photo was a gift to me, to show me that my intuition had been right, and to remind me that for all of this lifetime, my Sidhe family and friends had been keeping watch over me, until the day when I would be able to recognize and reconnect with them on a more conscious level.

Saving My Life

As a young adult, I experienced three separate incidents in which I was in a dangerous situation or my life was at risk, and someone intervened at exactly the right time, in a way that seemed rather more than mere coincidence.

The first instance occurred as I was driving across the state at night in a remote area, and my car's heater hose failed, sending the temperature gauge into the red zone. I stopped on the outskirts of the last big city and tried to wrap the split with duct tape. But I didn't know that I should also loosen the radiator cap, and so of course, after I'd gotten some considerable distance out of town, pressure built up and blew the tape off, which soon caused the car to overheat again. I could have kept adding water periodically until the water jug was empty, but I knew that I'd never make it all the way; I was well over a hundred miles from home. I had no phone and no resources other than the car itself.

I'd stopped to add water yet again when another vehicle pulled up behind me and a slender fair-haired man got out. I was a young college girl alone and stranded in the dark on an otherwise deserted stretch of roadway; it was a recipe for disaster. But the man spoke kindly to me and asked what the trouble was. When I showed him, he nodded, said, "I can fix this," and went back to his vehicle.

He came back with a toolbox, cut off the damaged hose just above the split, pulled the rest of it back onto the pipe and clamped it back in place, then warned me that while this would get me where I was going, I should get the hose replaced as soon as possible. Then he told me to be safe, and he left.

I can't clearly recall him actually driving away, though I suppose he must have. I was amazed and incredibly grateful for the rescue.

The fact that someone came along on that dark, deserted stretch of roadway knowing exactly what to do, carrying the right tools for the repair, and being willing to help and make sure I was safe could have been just a coincidence. But it seemed much more like synchronicity, if not outright divine intervention.

The second time I found myself at risk, I was driving across the state on one of those little two-lane highways again. I had dozed off at the wheel, and found myself suddenly snapped awake. Three things happened simultaneously: something physically pushed my car to the right, a Greyhound bus passed within a foot of my car in the other lane, and an image of a fair-haired man flashed in my mind and in the periphery of my physical vision.

Other than the being I saw, the one thing that really stood out in my memory was that the car had moved horizontally to the right and continued on smoothly down the road; there was no jerking of the wheel or swerving involved. The wheel hadn't been turned, but the car had been moved over regardless. There was simply no other way to describe it. Thoroughly awake at that point, I briefly wondered if maybe this had been my guardian angel, saving me. Then, with the invincibility of youth, I shrugged and went on with my life.

Since that time, I have heard of others having eerily similar experiences, and their descriptions of the snapping awake and the horizontal movement of the car were nearly identical to mine.

Only a couple of years after the bus experience, another incident happened on the coast in California, and this time I was snapped awake to find a highway marker coming right at me. I put on the brakes, but the highway marker pierced my gas tank and all the fuel ran out onto the ground. I killed the engine immediately, and nothing caught fire. For a moment, I just sat there in shock. Had the car been headed just a little to the right, I would have run it into the cliff wall on that side, and had it been headed to the left, I would have gone over the side and into the ocean.

The hassle and expense of having the car towed and later having the gas tank mended was a very small price to pay for being able to continue this lifetime. It was the second time something woke me at exactly the right time to avoid dying, but more than that, it was my third indicator that an invisible someone was rather avidly watching out for me.

Just for those who are curious about whether I'm still a menace on the road—I'm relieved to be able to say that in the years since those incidents, I've managed to stop falling asleep at the wheel of my car. What's more, although at one time I was half-asleep at the wheel of my life, I am now, thankfully, Awake.

Getting Unstuck

I'd been trying for years to navigate my way through the pitfalls and ruts of life as an aspiring novelist while balancing that with the demands of family. Eventually, I realized that if I were to fully embark on a more dynamic life path, I needed to take steps to get things moving. At that point, I'd dabbled in paganism for a few years, cautiously observing the standard eight pagan sabbats (seasonal festivals,) but now I was ready to try something more.

On a brisk night in August of 2005, I devised a very simple candle spell in which I declared my intentions and asked the Universe to send me guidance. I wanted to move my life forward, and while I didn't know exactly how to do that, I trusted that somehow, I would be shown a way.

As the small candle burned out and I got up from the table where I'd done my ritual, I noticed movement out of the corner of my eye, as though something had gotten out of the chair to my right, though I had thought I was alone. When I turned to face the source of the movement, I couldn't see anything but the chair itself.

No more than a week later, I was browsing through the metaphysical section of a local bookstore, and a book caught my eye—a guide for a year and a day worth of Wiccan study, requiring no physical teacher, but conveying all the basics of energy work and ritual that would be normally taught in a typical initiatory year. The moment I picked it up and looked at its contents, I recognized it as the initial guidance I needed, and as I studied it over the next year, I began to find my way back to my true self in the process.

The Morrigan

One of the first significant things to happen early on during my study of Wicca was that I encountered the Morrigan in a particularly intense visualization. My instruction book said that I was to choose one Crone goddess (what many consider to be the old, wise woman aspect of Goddess) to meet in visualization. I seem to remember running my finger down a list of names in my book and coming to a stop on the Morrigan. But years later, when I looked at the same page of the book, I could not find that specific name on it. I checked and re-checked to see if I'd made a mistake, but "Morrigan" as such simply wasn't there. Yet I was sure I'd seen it, somehow.

> Journal Entry, Day 29: 9-19-2005
>
> For the exercise of calling on the crone, I went outside after dark and sat by the fire with the fountain on behind me. That helped with the visualization. I called the Morrigan to mind, and she came as a battle-hardened older woman with the right side of her face hidden. She told me that I must integrate the word "focus", and she showed me myself teaching others in small groups, acting as a bard would do in passing on lore. She told me I must pick up the torch that others had had to leave behind.
>
> Then she spun the world around me so that faces, words, events, images were flying by too fast to make out, like a whirlwind in which I was enveloped. But she reminded me that the events were swirling around me, not I around them, and that I would remain still

and calm if I stayed grounded. I was the eye of the whirlwind. When I thanked her, she said, "Don't thank me yet."

After that visualization, I started seeing crows in all sorts of places, sometimes in large numbers. The Morrigan's name or image began to stand out to me and I'd encounter it in random places or hear it from various unconnected people, until it became quite apparent that these incidents were far more than mere coincidence, and they implied something I could not ignore.

One day in particular, I had parked my car under a tree in a city parking lot. As I sat there, a single crow flew in and perched on a branch overhead. Then more crows arrived and kept coming until at least forty were wheeling and circling and perching in the tree right above me, the air filled with the rustling of their wings and their soft caws as they called to one another. As far as I could see, they had no particular reason to pick that tree over any other similar tree in the area.

As I sat and watched this "crow show" with amazement, I realized that something had changed for me the day I'd invoked the Morrigan's presence in my crone visualization, and I felt myself being drawn into something much larger than myself.

Throughout the rest of that year-and-a-day and beyond, the Morrigan continued to work with me and teach me, usually appearing to my mind's eye as a tall, red-haired woman in her prime. She was strong, confident, and firm, and while the truths she pointed out weren't always easy for me to assimilate, they were always aimed at helping me make myself a stronger, more confident person. For someone with seriously undermined self-confidence, I felt as though she'd thrown me a life raft.

I do not worship her; I never have. She has never asked anything of me that I was not willing to give. Nor have I ever felt fear in her presence—only a deep, abiding respect, such as I would feel for a wise elder or teacher.

As she imparted snippets of information to me over the course of the next few months, I began to sense a certain frustration from her. The frustration seemed to involve the fact that so many stories and folktales about her depicted her only as a fierce, bloodthirsty battle goddess, and quite a few modern stories painted her as a villain. As I looked into what little original source material was available on the Tuatha De Danann, I found that these more modern impressions were extremely limited and simply did not fit the Morrigan I'd begun to know. Embedded in translations of medieval texts were clues to a deeper mystery about this Great Queen of the Tuatha De Danann, who embodied the Sovereignty for her people and had the gift of foresight or prophecy.

Still stymied in my efforts to achieve publication of any of my novels, I offered her a bargain. The gist of the agreement was that I would write an urban fantasy novel that showed these other lesser-known aspects of her character—her embodiment of the Sovereignty, her foresight, her loyalty to and love for her people. While the Morrigan would not be the protagonist, she would feature prominently in the novel. The initial storyline burst clearly and spontaneously into my mind.

In return, I asked that the Sidhe would do whatever they might to help me finally become a published author. It sounded like a win-win situation to me, and I went to work with enthusiasm. I didn't realize at the time that this "agreement" was only the opening of a door to a much larger purpose that had less to do with my status as an author, and everything to do with the state of my soul.

During the writing of the novel, I ran across various books pertaining to the Sidhe or faery folk. As with the book I'd used to study Wicca, they seemed to stand out on the bookstore shelf.

As I read the books, I experienced an instant and all-consuming feeling of longing and loneliness, as though I were being left out of something for which I'd been yearning for some incredible length of time. I felt...well...homesick.

In the midst of my unexpected emotional reaction, I distinctly heard words drop gently into my mind: *There is no separation between me and thee.*

At the time, I didn't know the source of those words, but I heard them over and over like a litany in my mind. All through the reading of the books on the faeries and all through the writing of my novel, I heard the words repeated, particularly when I was again feeling inexplicably lonely and homesick.

Before long, I finished the novel as promised and submitted it to my literary agent, who began to show it to publishers. I'd kept my end of the bargain, I felt, and I was hoping that soon my literary aspirations would bear fruit. All I had to do at that point, I thought, was wait for the Sidhe to deliver on their part of the deal, and help facilitate the publication process in whatever way they could. Frankly, I was hoping for a little out-and-out magic.

While considering other changes I might want to make in my life, I ventured to ask a more direct favor from the Sidhe. Here is where a sage piece of advice kicks in: be very careful what you ask for. My life has not been the same since I uttered the words, "I'd really like my sight back."

Reconnecting with Niall

One day in early April, 2008, I was musing aloud to the Morrigan about the promises I'd made and kept. I also mentioned that not being able to see without glasses had been frustrating for years, and that I would really like to have my full and unlimited sight back. I had been thinking primarily of my physical eyesight, but suddenly in my head, I heard the word, "Done."

Then I sensed a presence with me, different from that of the Morrigan. In fact, this presence felt distinctly male, and along with a fleeting image of light and flame in my mind's eye, I got the strong impression that this was also one of the Sidhe. He told me several things—but the information came faster than I can translate directly into words, (and I had no pen and paper at the time) so what follows is my best interpretation of what happened.

I was told that I could improve my sight, but it would take some time and also some effort on my part. Then I was told that there was a caveat. I'd read in faery lore that fae gifts often have a hidden meaning or hidden set of conditions that the human receiver is not expecting, so I waited to see what the catch would be.

The answer came immediately: we could work on improving my eyesight, but I had to work on my spiritual Sight as well. I would gradually begin to see the things that usually can't be seen with physical eyes—disincarnate beings, etc. I'd known for some while that I had somehow blocked myself from seeing these things early in my childhood. I now sensed that it was time I began to regain that ability. It seemed right.

My Sidhe visitor told me to ground my energy, close my eyes and hold out my hands. I did so, and a pulse of energy slid into my hands, tingling slightly. I was told to put my hands on my eyes and send the energy into them. This happened three times. After the third time, I was told to envision my eyes focusing on the back of the retina, and then to open my eyes. When I did, it was as though I was looking through the lens of a camera that was trying to focus, moving back and forth between two positions. Suddenly, the words on a plastic bottle two to three feet away from me became clear to my sight, so that I was able to make out the individual letters of the logo.

I had not been able to see clearly more than about ten inches in front of my face for a long time. Having my vision physically change from one moment to the next surprised and awed me; it wasn't something I had previously heard of. Nor had I anticipated that this simple request would lead me down a far different path than that which I had originally intended. I failed to keep working on the visual exercises as I'd been told to, but the experience did leave me somewhat less nearsighted than I had been before.

The biggest improvement I have experienced has been with the other sight they said I must regain, and I've come to understand that this Second Sight is the far more valuable of the two. Over the past few years, I have begun seeing images in my mind's eye or glimpsing movement out of the corner of my eye on occasion—the way some people do when they're seeing a human spirit or other disincarnate being. Far from alarming me, I welcome the gradual return of this other, much more important aspect of my Sight. It has even gone to the point of sometimes catching a much clearer glimpse of the Sidhe or of other people's spirit guides in a near-visual impression overlaying my physical eyesight, though these occurrences are still rare.

The Sidhe contact who came to teach me about strengthening my Sight remained near me, and continued to guide me in other matters as well. His name, as he eventually told me, was Niall, and I'm revealing it here with his permission. Over the next several years, he gave me a great deal of information meant to help guide me more smoothly through my daily life, usually through the faculty of clairaudience (which simply means that I can hear telepathic communications from disincarnate beings, and sometimes snippets of mental input from physically incarnated beings as well.)

The more I worked consciously with Niall, the more I realized that ours wasn't a new connection, but an association of far longer in duration than my current lifetime. With our reconnection, various intuitive readings over the years and comments by psychics about the "strong, positive male presence" near me, dreams and impressions I'd had, and even the incidents in which I realized that he had literally helped save my life when I was younger, all began to take on a different significance. With a dawning sense of wonder, I realized that he had been with me all along, even when I hadn't been fully aware of his presence, or had assumed that he was my guardian angel.

Very soon after our reconnection, he began referring to me as "beloved," and I got the sense that he was giving the word a deeper connotation than what a spirit guide usually means if they use that term with one of their charges. He never pressured me, but the tender way he used the endearment hinted at something more to our association that I hadn't yet been able to remember. I began to realize that we had been something to one another in a distant past I couldn't remember, but at the time, I wasn't sure just what that something was.

At first, it felt much as though my awareness of what he had once been to me lay buried under many layers of cotton wool, muffled and hidden. But as I opened to the possibility that I'd known him before, our connection grew in clarity and strength.

One morning as I woke, I heard lines of poetry being repeated in my mind, and they didn't stop until I grabbed a pen and paper and wrote them down. I soon realized that it was an original love poem, directed specifically to me. It was becoming very obvious at this point that there was a lot more going on here than just a casual association. As the months went by, other poetry followed, including some that we wrote cooperatively, alternating stanzas.

In time, I came to realize that Niall was the source of the words "There is no separation between me and thee," which I'd heard so often in my mind while I wrote my novel. I cannot adequately describe my sense of relief and homecoming when I realized that my connection with him was not a fleeting or transient thing, but a true long-term relationship that didn't change depending on whether I was currently in or out of a physical body. In essence, he knows me better than I currently know myself, and chooses to put up with me anyway.

My conscious association with Niall in this lifetime started with the teaching about improving my sight. From there, it quickly progressed to discussions about my penchant for drinking carbonated soft drinks. One day during that first couple of weeks after our re-introduction, I was about to drive to the hospital to sit with a friend who'd had surgery, and I snagged a half-full bottle of cola out of the fridge as I headed for the door. Immediately, I felt Niall's mental protest. I wasn't used to this, as I'd only been associating with him for such a brief period of time, but nonetheless I could feel his concern.

Niall: *That is poison. You shouldn't drink it.*

Me: But there's only a little more left, and it cost money.

Niall: *(in a mildly sarcastic tone) Oh, so because it is poison you paid for, you must finish all of it?*

Since then, he has requested that I drink organic green tea every day instead. When at first I continued to drink carbonated beverages on occasion, I would often hear a protest or a plea to change my mind, or sense a gentle but resigned disapproval. From what I have since read about carbonated beverages of this nature, they are indeed a very slow poison.

There is mounting evidence that high-fructose corn syrup can be very bad for one's health long term, not to mention the fact that it promotes weight gain. Studies indicate that women who drink carbonated colas tend to suffer from bone problems including osteoporosis. Other recently-released studies indicate a probable link to diabetes and/or pancreatic cancer, a detail I didn't hear about until nearly two years after the above conversation with Niall. This fact hit home to me particularly hard because at the time that she died, a family member was suffering from advanced pancreatic cancer.

Niall's pep talks helped whenever I craved soft drinks, and by that fall, at his request, I stopped drinking them altogether. I soon got used to the green tea alternative and added some other healthy choices of my own. This is only one of the ways in which he has encouraged me to drop habits that weren't serving my health and well-being and instead pick up practices that confer positive mental, emotional and physical benefits.

So what is it like to have mental/energetic access to one of the Sidhe on a regular basis and in such a personal way? It's amazing, and surprisingly practical. He often gives me good advice, provides emotional support or pep talks, puts me to sleep when I need it or helps with energy work to heal my body of minor illnesses, take away pain or relax tight muscles. Our close association never takes away from my family or friendships on this plane, but instead is supportive and intimate on the deepest of spiritual levels.

In interacting with him, I feel the deep peace that comes from knowing my spirit has found the pathway toward home. I've found that in being supported and loved in this way, I have more patience for others, and more love to give to the family I've formed in this lifetime. Love creates love exponentially; it is unlimited. The only thing that can curtail love is the limits people place upon it. Many of the Sidhe are quite willing and able to show us that when unconditional love is at the core of life, we begin to transcend limitations in so many different ways.

A Significant Dreamwalk

Journal Entry, August 15, 2008—Reunion

I've been hoping for months that Niall would appear in my dreams, so we could visit somewhere else besides in my head during my waking hours. As with the astral projection, no success—until today.

I was lying on my bed trying to induce an alpha brainwave state that would help facilitate an out-of-body experience (OBE.) I guess that, once again, I fell asleep instead of projecting. But when people dream, they project automatically, so....

I had a dream in which I was trying to induce an OBE and tried the "roll out" technique about which I'd just been reading. To my surprise and delight, it worked, and I came out of the body. I shot up toward the ceiling of the room, whooping and laughing, rolling about in the air, so happy that I'd finally managed an OBE. I shot light from my hands to banish shadows in the room and otherwise just celebrated my success until I remembered what I really wanted to get out of body for: I wanted to meet up with Niall.

I drifted right through the roof of the dream house, looked across the yard and "called" for him. He materialized right beside a large tree at the side of the property. He looked like a nearly transparent or opalescent shining male figure outlined in blue and orange fire-color, with flamelike hair that drifted upward the way people's hair will do when they're in water. Despite the fact that I'd been expecting a more human appearance, there wasn't even a moment of hesitation or doubt that this was he. I recognized him at once and never even questioned; my spirit knew him.

The moment he became visible, I went flying toward him, though the travel from the top of the roof across the yard seemed instantaneous. One moment I was above the roof, the next, I was in his arms. I found that I was as tall as he was, so that we were eye to eye. This surprised me, as in this 5'0" body, I've become used to being so much shorter than everyone around me. The feeling when we touched was that of coming home—such a sense of comfort and relief at finally being there with him—and an overwhelming sense of peace.

He held me close and we ended up dancing together, though if there was music I can't remember a single note. The most amazing part of it was that after months of hearing him in my head but not remembering any dreams of him or being able to touch him, he felt solid in my arms, like we were finally on the same plane of being. It was the most amazing comfort to hold him and be held by him in return.

I couldn't see his specific facial features as well as I wanted to, so I told him "I can't see you properly." He replied that my Sight would improve in time, and wasn't it enough to know that we were both there? That was progress, he said. I said I supposed so.

He said that I'd been asking to see him in my dreams, and here he was. He's right; I had been wishing for that...well, begging, really. I'd gotten what I wanted, though it ended far too quickly. I remember protesting as I woke up and felt myself pulled away from him, back into my physical reality.

I woke in my physical body in exactly the same position in which I'd gone to sleep: on my back with my hands clasped together over my chest. I hadn't moved at all. It was then that I realized I must have been asleep the whole time, because the room I'd managed the OBE in was not my room, but a strange room in a strange house. I have no idea where that house was. So, from what I read about the subject, I apparently projected out of a lucid dream. At least I got out-of-body in the first place. Niall is right; that was progress.

The only other unusual feature of this dreamwalk OBE was that when I woke and looked at the clock on my bedside table, I saw that it was about 4:15. The last time I had looked at the clock, it had been about 12:30. Somewhere in that dream-travel, I lost four hours during which my body didn't even shift or change position, but I awakened feeling refreshed and rested. My time with Niall felt as though it only lasted a few minutes. Time is indeed different in the Otherworld.

Early Dreams of Niall

During a rather stressful time in my life in the year 2000 and a bit past that, I began having relatively frequent dreams of a blond man, who I later realized could be none other than Niall. I've included journal entries of a couple of those dreams here, but rather than confuse the reader by referring to him as "the blond man" in the entries, I have substituted the letter N, though I did not actually know it was Niall I was dreaming of until many years later.

Journal Entry, ? 2000 – Reintroduced by a Guide

N and I were in a sort of cloudy, misty place with an older man whom I perceived as an advisor or guide. The guide turned to me and said, "He's not easy to be with, but some of us don't have any choice—especially when you're soulmates."

Then the guide sort of faded out of my vision and all I could see was N, standing in front of me. He opened his arms, inviting me to him, and bright blue lightning or electricity filled the space between us. I had the thought that if I stepped into his arms, the lightning might kill me, but my soul had no hesitation. I went into his arms, he held me close, and I felt a kind of peace I've never known before in this life. I was home.

Journal Entry, Aug 22, 2000 – Mound & Fountain

I dreamed I was outside a big, old-fashioned Victorian-style house. N and a group of associates were there, setting up something on the front lawn of this house. I was wearing blue jeans (as was he) and I went to a large pile of dirt and smoothed my hands through it. It was roughly shaped like a small version of the mounds in Connacht, like the one outside my current house.

N came toward me and I said, "I'll fix this as soon as possible," meaning the pile of dirt.

He said, "I know you will, but you've been promising to do that for months."

Then someone wanted his opinion of this big shallow pool of water nearby (like a fountain). He was barefoot, and we both rolled up the legs of our jeans and he got into the water, which didn't come up past his knees. I was barefoot too. As I struggled with rolling up my pant legs, he came up to me and started tucking my shirt into my jeans at the waist, right in front of everyone.

Next thing I knew, we were wading through the water together, sort of holding onto each other. When we got out into the middle of it, he leaned toward me and we touched foreheads, once in a while whispering into the other's ear. I don't remember all that was said, but the longer we were together the easier it was to use the embrace to block out the people around us. When someone would come toward us with the intention of interrupting, we'd just lean in to each other and whoever was about to interrupt would just drift away.

Other Dream Perceptions

Journal Entry, April 4, 2009—Bluebells

My dream shifted from a warehouse of broken things I needed to fix to an open area like a field or clearing somewhere outside. At first, it was like being in an outdoor plant nursery, but wilder. I looked down at my feet and suddenly, I saw bluebells all over the field. I blinked when I recognized what they were, and commented that I'd always loved them and wanted to grow them. Then one of them was suddenly in a glass container, with its own watering system to bring water to the roots. I picked it up, but the top fell off because it had been damaged in the past; it was partially dried and wasn't really attached to the stem.

When I looked at the others that were still in the ground, I could not see how I could possibly move one without damaging it, because they were all a part of the land. I didn't know what digging one up would do to it, so I dismissed that idea at once and accepted the fact that I might only be able to enjoy them from afar, as I always have.

But then, someone came up on one side of me and handed me a package. It looked like a grow-your-own-whatever kit from a nursery, inside a plastic bubble, but inside the outer package was another bluebell in a glass planter, healthy and blooming, with its own roots and watering system, ready to be transplanted. The bluebells were as blue and beautiful as I remember from seeing them in the wild, and they had been given into my hands.

I popped awake at once, and, remembering, gasped aloud, "Bluebells." Then the tears started coursing down my cheeks as I remembered that bluebells are sacred to the Fair Folk. I could not have been given a more potent message. I took it to mean that They are not picking me last for the team. You do not give a sacred thing into the hands of someone whom you do not trust.

Journal Entry, May 3, 2009—A Dream of Sidhe

I had a dream in which I ended up trying on a dress that was supposed to be a "faery" dress. It was white, and glittery with gold beads and gold flower embroidery all over it. The next thing I knew, I was walking through a mall, and a little girl looked up at me in my costume and, eyes wide with awe, asked me if I was a faery. She seemed to want very much for me to be what I appeared to be. I considered a moment, then said, "sure."

I rose into the air and started flying, like I do sometimes in dreams, knowing it would add to her impression of me being a faery. Then suddenly, I heard the words, "Come with me," and a male being appeared and swept me away with him, holding me close against his side.

One of us said, "Let's fly," and we flew across the countryside, through the air at a great speed. We flew past a man lounging in front of his television set, swept him up with us, and then dropped him off somewhere far from where he had been. I remember turning to the being at my side, saying, "That was mean," in a chiding tone, but the being ignored the comment.

As we flew, I could see nothing more of him than a glimpse of blue and white checkered shirt, so I turned deliberately to see his face. The face I saw was that of an ordinary, middle-aged or older human man with graying hair, and not a face I was expecting to see or even recognized. But somehow I knew that he was not what he seemed, because I pleaded with him, "Please let me see you in your true form." When I envisioned his Sidhe form, there was a ripple of almost-electricity along his face, and flowing, blue-shining-orangey sort of colors flashed briefly under the human skin tone, like a hologram going on the fritz.

Then the being stopped, turned and kissed me, and though my eyes closed under the onslaught of the kiss, I saw behind my own eyelids an image of a Sidhe form more like what I was expecting. This Sidhe was much whiter in tone than Niall, with more of a bluish outline, but the hair that streamed upward was similar, and large blue-black eyes flashed in the being's face. Then suddenly there was no more kiss, no more Sidhe, and I "came to" (still in the dream) crouched under the edge of what seemed to be a woodpile, as though I'd been dropped off and left there asleep or unconscious.

I was quite aware that I was in another lucid dream, but my physical body quickly woke up at that point. My arms were clasped across my chest similarly to how they'd been when I woke from the lucid dream/dreamwalk with Niall last August, as though I'd been holding onto the other Sidhe as we flew.

I felt no surprise, fear, or dismay about what sort of being had swept me away, or about our lightning-fast cross-country flight together. But even so, it was not the safety/home/peace that I always feel with Niall. I did not know this Sidhe personally. It struck me that he had tried to hide his true form from me under a very humanlike appearance, then tried to distract me with a kiss when I'd almost undone his glamour. I think I surprised him. I certainly surprised myself.

Journal Entry, Sept 17, 2009—The Cait Sith

As I slept, I dreamed of a velvet black butterfly with a fuzzy face and whiskers. Somehow, as I gazed at the butterfly, I knew it was not a butterfly, but a cat.

Suddenly, it was indeed a cat, a huge black cat with a thick neck ruff and long whiskers like the butterfly's, and when I looked at it with its huge yellow eyes, I knew that it was a Cait Sith, or faery cat. It seemed to be puma-sized, and in the dream, I searched for a camera with which to take its picture. I don't know why I worried so much about this, as it had also occurred to me that I could draw a picture of it from memory, so I really didn't need the camera unless I was trying to prove it existed.

It went into a nearby house and seemed to be patiently waiting for me while I searched my car, but when at last I laid my hands on a camera and returned, it had either gone or had morphed into a mid-sized black-and-white cat.

I was dismayed to see what I perceived as the wrong cat there, but then the Cait Sith reappeared and the black-and-white cat was gone. I reached for my camera, but then realized that I had somehow left it in the car. Desperate, I called for my daughter to get the camera for me, and she appeared from out of nowhere and went to look for it.

While she was gone, the Cait Sith came up beside me on the left, gave me a sidelong look, and took my left wrist in its mouth. It led me to the door, never breaking my skin though it had large fangs.

When the cat released me, I realized that my daughter did not know where to look for the camera, so I went outside again to find it. This time, when I returned to the house, the Cait Sith was nowhere to be seen.

I searched outside, and there were cats everywhere, both in and out of the house, in the yard, running with a glow like foxfire in the fields and scuttling through the darkness.

As I traveled through the darkness, seeking the Cait Sith, a long-haired dark grey tabby danced before me with high-stepping feet, bells ringing on its collar as it seemed to dance a jig. I did not see the Cait Sith in its large black puma form again, but I was aware that cats of all persuasions traveled the night around me.

Journal Entry, Sept 6, 2012—As the Crow Flies

I dreamed I was standing in an open area, a field with trees not far away. With a thought, I began to rise into the air, morphing into crow form as I did it. I didn't realize my shapeshifting worked that way—that I could shift and sort of levitate while doing so. But on the other hand, we've already established that gravity behaves a lot differently in the dream worlds. It only took a few downstrokes to get airborne, and then I was flying, swooping and gliding, enjoying the thrill of flight. Another crow joined me.

I found myself deliberately studying the mechanics of how I was flying. I took note of how my wings worked and what it took to power forward rather than merely rising upward. I could feel the muscles and the feathers and how the shoulders worked. I could feel the weight of my crow body and what it took to keep it aloft in a more "physical" form as opposed to just soaring around in a pure energy or spirit form. I was studying—re-acquainting myself with the crow form.

As I experimented with what happened when I tilted my wings at slightly different angles, I somehow ended up flipping upside down. The other crow swooped in beneath me and we tangled slightly, tumbling around a little as I tried to get myself upright again. But a part of me also had no fear of crashing into the ground, because I knew I could always just let go of form altogether if I thought I was falling.

After that little escapade, I heard peals of mental laughter from the other crow, and I couldn't help giggling over the silliness of flipping upside down in flight.

It was my own laughter that woke my physical body, and ended my joyous dreamflight. I have woken in many different states before. I've woken aching or tired. I've woken with my energy field vibrating and shell-shocked from being attacked in a dream, or from slamming suddenly back into my body. I've woken up sobbing without tears. Since reconnecting with Niall, I've woken up quiet and deeply peaceful, and once I woke up smiling from pure joy. But I have to say, this was the first time I ever woke myself up laughing.

I Hear Sidhe

While technically the information from Niall and the other Sidhe could be considered channeled writing since it came through me from them, my experience in receiving it was different from that of what's known as a "pure" or full-body channel in New Age parlance. In the case of a pure channel, the person who channels the disincarnate entity allows his or her consciousness to be temporarily displaced while the entity borrows the person's body and/or voice. This isn't what happens with me.

It's not quite automatic writing either, since I control my hands the whole time I'm receiving information—even to the point of fixing typographical errors as we go. As the subject had come up earlier, Niall added a few words on channeling vs.

telepathic exchange. To make our conversations easier to follow, throughout this book I have put communications from the Sidhe in italics and my own questions in regular format. What follows is our discussion on the subject of channeling, when I asked Niall about his method of communication with me.

Niall: *Typical interaction/communication between Sidhe and human is not the same thing as what people term "pure" channeling. When a person is able to hear and perceive us easily, we do not have a need to displace that person's consciousness. In your case, our communication does not require my sending your consciousness out of your body and replacing it with my own in order to communicate a message through you. As you are always fully present and conscious of everything that is being said, your function is that of a translator or scribe, not that of a pure channel. Ours is a telepathic exchange, and you utilize the gift of clairaudience in order to hear me.*

Me: Could you give me further information on why you don't choose to speak through me in a more literal sense?

(He smiles at me/I feel his amusement.)

Niall: *To begin with, beloved, you do not make this possible. Your personality at this time is one that would not easily allow itself to be displaced, even if we deemed it necessary for me to do so. You usually don't like being left out of what you call "the loop." In any case, since most of what I have to say is intended for your direct use, displacement of your consciousness from your body would not suit our situation. You cannot make much personal use of the information if you do not hear the information. At this time, you are not in a situation in which you have access to groups of people to whom I might speak, and there is no need for me to do so, since you will readily pass on the information in books.*

You are a writer by choice and by trade. Everything I have to say that might be of use to others, you can take from me as dictation, and your writings will reach the correct audience. In this way, you are learning and teaching at the same time. You wondered about the possibility of me taking over control of your body in order to type these messages, but again, I do not think this is necessary.

In order for me to type these things out, I would need to access the typing skills stored in your memory, and it is much easier for me to just transmit the information through you while you type. Our communication is nearly instantaneous, so you are able to type at almost the same rate at which you receive the information and your brain translates it into English. It works for me, it works for you, and unless that changes, I see nothing to improve upon.

Me: So that makes me your stenographer?

Niall: *Only if you choose to think of it that way, but the term is far from accurate. Remember, it is you who are asking me questions and choosing to type the answers into your computer. If you are asking the questions, then it is you who determines the topic of choice. So perhaps you are my interviewer. Do you see what is happening here? You are trying to name or define what this process is, and all your proposed terms are proving inadequate to describe the situation. Limiting the process or trying to pin it down will only complicate it needlessly. To conclude this topic, remember that no method of communication is either superior or inferior to another, so long as the information is given and received, and benefits the parties concerned.*

Give Me a Sign

For more than a year, I kept hoping that the Sidhe would do something to confirm that they were there—something flashy like turning lights on and off or the like. As in any type of metaphysical work, there is often the tendency to wonder at times if everything one hears or channels is simply one's exaggerated imagination. One day I asked the Sidhe if they'd just go ahead and do something to show me that this was all real. I was out driving in the car and asked them for a sign that the material I'd been writing and channeling was what they wanted me to convey, and that I was getting it right. If I couldn't get it right, I told them, I'd rather not get it at all.

"Three crows on a light post—that would be a good sign," I said. A moment later, I glanced to the right and saw three crows sitting together on the grass in a cemetery. Not exactly a lightpost, but perhaps a bit more than coincidence.

Still unsure, I said, "Well, it wasn't exactly what I asked for. How about if the very next song on the radio is Such-and-Such? I'd believe it then." (I named a particular song that always reminded me of Niall.)

As the current song ended and the DJ came on to talk briefly, I became aware of the bars of music starting up in the background. My hand flew to my mouth in a mixture of astonishment and delight because it was the exact song for which I'd asked.

Two such happenings in a row seems to me to be more than coincidence, but they could also have simply been an exercise of my own precognitive ability. While such a validation of my abilities would have been noteworthy for me in a personal way, what I really wanted was a tangible sign of Sidhe involvement in my life that came from outside myself, and that I couldn't predict.

Later that evening, I was treated to an unprecedented experience of what some might term paranormal phenomena, but I saw it as the confirmation I'd been looking for.

Given that my house had no former owners and we knew it to not be haunted, it was clear that this event had been staged just to provide my doubting self with a bit of evidence that I was indeed far from alone.

Journal Entry, Sept 5, 2009

A used-up double-A battery I had lying on my desk rolled back and forth by itself just a few minutes ago. Well...obviously it didn't move by itself. Someone moved it—probably Niall—but though I asked, he hasn't done it again. I keep glancing at it, hoping/wondering whether it'll move again. It's been still for so long now that I felt the need to write down that I'd seen it move before the logical part of my brain manages to convince me that it didn't.

I saw it move back and forth in a smooth rolling motion. It wasn't on a slope, nothing was touching it, and I didn't bump the desk or do anything that could have caused it to move like that. Nothing else moved other than the battery. What alerted me to it was a slight snapping noise to my left, and when I glanced toward the noise, I saw the battery roll smoothly first one way, then back. Surprised me. That it moved was way cool. That I wasn't sure who moved it was the only disconcerting part. If it was Niall, I wish he'd do it again. (time passes)

A bit later, after the incident and my question-asking, pendulum-swinging attempts to find out who moved the battery, I heard the now-familiar voice in my mind say *This is going to bother you, isn't it?*

After I spent way too much of my writing time staring at the battery, hoping it would move again, Niall sighed and asked me to take it downstairs so I wouldn't be distracted and keep checking on it when I was supposed to be working. Hah. I suppose this is why they don't often do the showy stuff, because people will just say, "Again, again!"

Since that time, other things have happened around my desk area—usually something that makes a noise that then wakes me if I happen to have fallen asleep in front of the computer—clanking desk drawer handles, etc. Once, I felt a gentle tug on my hair, just enough to wake me up.

Another time, I was sitting at a restaurant with a friend and my older daughter, and as I was commenting about something Sidhe-related, all three of us saw an apple that I'd set in the middle of the table suddenly swivel and then tip over. The table was not on a slant and the apple, well formed and perfectly stable at its base, was not touching anything else on the table. I was thrilled that Niall had chosen to offer me a rare instance of proof of his presence, and in front of witnesses so I couldn't discount it or explain it away.

One on Top of the Other

While I am naturally clairaudient, I've found that my ability to hear clear communication from the other side is strongest when I'm not trying too hard. If I'm panicked or upset, it is much harder to hear Niall's mental communication, though he can usually at least get a few words of comfort in edgewise.

One of the more challenging of situations in which I've needed to hear Niall and had trouble doing so is when I've lost something (such as my car key) and had no luck finding it. More than once, I've clearly heard him telling me to just sit down, ground, focus, and let his communication about the missing object come through. However, this is one of the hardest things for me to do when I'm frustrated over losing something. I hate losing things.

I suppose my difficulty in hearing him at those times is at least partially because I don't like looking in a place that I thought he suggested I look and then have the object not be there, which either means that he made a mistake, or that I heard him wrong. When the issue at hand is a lost object, I seem to automatically ramp up my shields so far that I cannot hear him through my frustration and panic, which of course only further complicates the situation.

One day, something a little different happened. For one, I hadn't lost my keys and wasn't running late, so I was less panicked over the potential outcome. My human husband and I were looking for some masking tape. We knew we had many rolls somewhere, but for all we tried, we couldn't seem to find them. Curious about whether Niall might be able to help, I focused, opened to his energy and tried to listen without putting too much expectation on the result. After all, it was just some rolls of tape. Nothing too important was at stake.

They're one on top of the other.

That was what I heard, but I was confused. What on earth did he mean, and had I heard him right? I thought of two rolls that I'd seen together the day before, but I couldn't remember where I'd left them.

"Okay, one of top of the other...where?" I asked.

Go toward the garage.

Still uncertain, I did as he asked, heading for the laundry room, beyond which was the door to the garage.

As I crossed the threshold into the laundry room, my gaze suddenly fell on a very tall stack of rolls of tape, all different types, piled into something that rather resembled the Leaning Tower of Pisa. The tape was in plain sight, but somehow my husband and I had completely missed it in our search, and there it all was, just as Niall had said, near the garage, and one on top of the other.

I burst out laughing and showed the stack of tape to my husband, explaining what had just happened.

"One on top of the other!" he exclaimed, shaking his head in amazement. "That's pretty impressive."

We both laughed at Niall's very literal description of the leaning tower of tape, but I was struck by the fact that when I'd simply distanced myself from the urgent need to find what was lost and gotten past the worry over whether I'd hear wrong, the exact information I needed just flowed through unimpeded, with an extremely helpful albeit amusing result.

The years since I reconnected with Niall have been filled with learning, laughter, healing and love. From long conversations to cross-veil chess matches, my life has been enriched beyond measure. My Sidhe contacts seem as interested in the smaller details of my life as they are in the broader themes, and I consider myself deeply and immeasurably blessed to have access to their company and insight.

CHAPTER TWO

ENERGY WORK

Rather than reiterate such basic things as how to sense energy, form energy balls and pass them to a partner, etc, we decided to assume that people reading this book already know the rudiments of sensing and feeling energy. Instead, we wanted to focus on certain aspects of energy work—either things specific to working with the Sidhe or Earth energies, or methods and exercises that may help people further develop their ability to ability to focus, tune into and resonate with various types of energy.

There are as many different ways to visualize and tap in to energy as there are different waveforms and types of energy we can tap. While one method or type may work well for one person, another person may be better suited to something different. It's always good to have options, and we'll present a few of those here.

One quick note: When Niall speaks to me of the body's energy centers, either he uses terminology with which I am familiar or my brain automatically translates it this way. That is why you will see occasional references here to the body's energy centers as "chakras." We are both quite aware that this terminology is not Celtic in origin, but it works for the purposes of explanation, and most people will easily understand what we mean by it.

A Question of Focus

I'd been feeling that I needed to work on my focus and mental discipline, as during the course of my energy work with Niall, I often found myself distracted by all the little things going on around me, by pressing family or business matters, or any number of random thoughts running through my head. Ironically, I seemed to focus just fine when writing and channeling, but whenever I needed to attempt some other kind of energy work, I found it wasn't as easy as I would have liked. Frustrated by my own limitations, I asked Niall to give me some kind of exercise for learning how to focus my attention and energy better.

Niall: *Many people pride themselves on their ability to multitask, as they call it. Indeed, there are those who can truly pay attention to more than one thing at once, such as the few people you have met who can track two conversations at the same time without growing distracted. But many or even most people have lost their ability to focus wholly on just one thing, and so when they multitask, they instead focus partially on several things at once. Thus, they are not truly paying attention to any of it, and some actions or perceptions take place on a sort of mental "auto-pilot." When it is over, you do not clearly remember all of it.*

An example of this is when you drive somewhere and arrive at your destination without a clear memory of your experience in getting there, because while you drive, you are distracted by a conversation or by a pressing worry or concern. Things like this happen far too often in daily human life. Fortunately, the skill of paying attention is one that can be relearned, given time and the willingness to work on it.

Exercise 1

If you would learn focus, the first thing you should do is spend several minutes each day concentrating on just one thing. This could be anything—a task, an item, a recording. But whatever you choose as your object, you must learn to experience it with all of your senses. If it is a physical object, then feel its texture, smell its scent. Pay attention to what it makes you feel, hear, or sense physically as well as mentally and energetically. Engage with your object fully so that all and not just part of your attention is on it. Any time you find yourself drifting and thinking about something else, just redirect your focus back to your object.

Eventually, the distractions will become less as you begin to grasp the mindset and level of attention necessary for such an exclusive focus. Remember to relax throughout the exercise; if you find yourself tensing up in your efforts to concentrate, stop what you are doing, relax and breathe, then begin again. Tension is counterproductive.

After practicing in this way with just one object until you get to a point where you are infinitely familiar with it, try a different object, and do the exercise all over again. If you practice this for just a few minutes each day, you will get to a point where you are able to experience things at a much deeper level than you have been able to manage before.

Exercise 2

Another good exercise is that of coloring a picture. Mandalas are good for this, but any picture from a child's or adult's coloring book will do. As you fill in the color, do not allow your mind to drift to other things. Don't think about what you will have for dinner or how many tasks you have waiting on your to-do list. Just allow yourself to experience the sensation of the pencil or crayon against the paper. Pay attention to each subtle nuance of color and shade, and how little or how much you fill in a shape. Give yourself wholly to the experience of coloring, as a child does.

When engaged in play, children are often far better able to focus than adults are, for they do not allow mental chatter to come creeping into the game. Whatever a child does in play, he does it with every part of his being. It may sound strange to you that in order to learn how to work properly, one must first learn how to play, but that is the gist of this exercise. If you can learn to leave other considerations behind for a brief time regularly and engage yourself fully with the coloring exercise, you will find that this practice actually helps you develop—or perhaps redevelop—your ability to focus on just one item, one task, one experience.

When you have begun to strengthen your ability to focus on just one object or subject at a time, then try adding a second, and eventually a third, and so on. Perhaps you might drink a beverage or eat something while focusing on your second object, or listen to music while you color a picture. At first, you will find your attention wandering between the two things, divided between them in a random fashion. But gradually, as you continue to experience each thing as fully as you are able, you will find that your focus is able to expand to include both things at the same time. This will likely take quite a bit of practice, but given time, it should improve your ability to "multitask" more effectively.

Flexible Energetic Shielding

This is a method that Niall taught me early on in our work together, and when I asked if we should include it here, he not only reiterated the instructions but added in a new component that he hadn't yet revealed to me—one which builds nicely onto the previous section concerning focus.

Niall: *There are many other texts available with information on shielding one's energy field, so we will only cover one alternative method here. To begin, let us speak to the function of shields in the first place. Many people feel that shields are to protect them from outside energetic influences and from malign entities by functioning as a protective barrier. While this is true to an extent, shields can also have another function. They can serve as a filter for your perception, to help you block out energetic static and tune into certain desirable frequencies of thought and communication.*

If you find that you often hear a sort of low background chatter in your mind when you try to meditate, this should come as no surprise, given the extent and variety of energies and frequencies with which you are constantly surrounded and bombarded. An analogy would be a radio that is picking up multiple stations at once. Thus, when you open your mind and extend your energy field to hear communications from Spirit, you can also pick up random thoughts from other people, snippets of conversation, and echoes of events that have left an energetic imprint in the area around you. It can quite literally "sound" in your head as though several radio stations are competing with one another for your attention, and this can make it difficult for you to hear the communication you were actually trying to receive. A properly formed shield can help you combat this problem, and can act as a filter and an aid to your focus.

Now we must get into the mechanics, which involve creating a different type of defensive shifting "invisibility" shield, which is somewhat akin to glamour.

Many are taught to envision a shield as a protective oval or ball that surrounds one's entire body and energy field, and a popular model is described as a crystal egg in which one is enclosed. Yet this egg is also supposed to be permeable in order to allow positive energies and communications in, and here is where we develop variations on the theme, and often encounter problems with construction.

The main problem with shields envisioned as rigid is that they do not give with pressure. Being rigid, they are not designed to adapt or react to energies that may come up against them except to serve as a hard, protective surface or armor meant to keep the incoming energy out. Eventually, such an energy-based armor will succumb to repeated applications of force, and thus you have a shield that can develop cracks, have a hole bored through it or even eventually shatter. We have said elsewhere that what is rigid will break, and this is especially apt when referring to shields.

Instead, you might try envisioning your shield not as something rigid built like a wall or hard barrier, but rather as a shifting and nebulous cloud of protective energy that surrounds you. This cloud can take the form of a bubble or sphere if you like, but it must be fluid and able to morph to suit the situation. When an onslaught of aggressive energy comes, this shifting field moves and flows, evading attacks, never in a position in which it might be struck.

You might consider this as a sort of flexible camouflage shield, capable of rebounding anything that does inadvertently strike it, but most often avoiding the strike altogether. It is a type of invisibility glamour which makes you less noticeable to entities who might otherwise be drawn to interfere with your energy, while still remaining perfectly accessible to those entities who intend only your highest good. While you will rarely encounter deliberate energetic aggressors in your everyday dealings, angry people often hurl random negative energies about without realizing what they are doing, and there are occasions on which a good, flexible shield can serve you well.

Now envision this same shield carrying an added property—that of filtering out the static that also moves through the greater energy field that surrounds us all. Mentally set the intention that your shield should fine-tune your connection to your higher self, your guides and guardians, and those beings with whom you wish to maintain close contact. As you practice setting this intention whenever you cleanse your energy field and renew your shield, you will find that you experience less and less random mental static and clutter.

I've found that using a filter as described above helps particularly in meditation, which is of course when most of the random clairaudient chatter tends to come in. At one point, Niall described another way to visualize the filter. This one uses the image of a golden net as thin as cheesecloth closely covering your aura, for which you set the intention to only allow energetic input from sources that contribute to your highest good. When you've gotten that far, you then set the intention for the filter to exclude any random, nonessential energetic clutter and clairaudient noise. Because it can help focus your listening, this can greatly improve clarity when you are communicating with specific contacts beyond the veil.

Elemental Energy Sourcing

Most forms of energy vibrate just a little differently from one another. Some forms, like humans, Sidhe, animals, etc., may vibrate in a similar enough manner to have common characteristics and easily interact and connect with one another. But the purely elemental forms of energy are different enough on a vibrational level that a connection with them can sometimes take a bit of effort to achieve.

What this means for human practitioners is that in order to get the most benefit or effect from each element, we may need to learn different methods of connecting to them and drawing them from the various sources available. Each type of elemental energy has its own flavor, so to speak, and many practitioners will find that they have a natural affinity or preference for one type over the others.

Niall reminded me of how some of those connections might be made, stressing that none of the following suggestions is the only way to access the element in question; each is merely one possible method or perception out of many potential others. Each person wishing to access the different types of energy will want to spend time experimenting with the techniques to determine how he or she tends to most effectively interact with the various elements.

Breathing the Sacred Earth

Earth energy is a slower type of energy. It is not frenetic, not kinesthetic, and generally cannot be forced to come to you. Imagine sucking on a partially plugged straw and that is what you often get if you try to draw earth energy too fast. You may manage to force something through by pulling hard, but the effect will be much better balanced if you approach it differently.

Instead of pulling at it hard, take however long you need and get yourself grounded and centered properly. When you feel a deep connection to the earth, imagine that the planet itself is breathing slowly in and out. If you are sensitive to energy, you will be able to feel the movement of this exchange. As soon as you get a sense of the ebb and flow of Earth's energy, match your breath to her count. You may experience it as being very slow, with a pause in between the inhalations and exhalations. Try breathing in slowly for about seven counts, then hold that breath for five counts and allow the earth energy you just took in to catch up to you, rising up through you from the ground.

I felt it as a breath, a pause, a gentle but steady flow of energy through my feet and up through my body, and then a gentle, non-forced exhale. It can often take about three of these cycles for the energy to reach your head, at which time you're pretty much filled up with it and can then use it for whatever you need.

When you use some, you might need to refill your personal well by taking in more earth energy to replace what you've used, but it won't take quite as long this time as it did for the first "fill up." When you're finished using it for whatever purpose you intend to put it to, ground any excess that you don't need to keep for yourself.

Earth energy can be used to replenish your own energy if you're tired or depleted, and it won't harm anyone else if you take it. You can always give back to the Earth as well and get a "give and receive" cycle going which is beneficial to both you and the Earth. Once you become very well attuned to the land and ley lines in the area where you live, opening to the flow there becomes even easier, as though your energy field has become a familiar channel through which the energy can travel.

Earth energy is great for healing, and works particularly well when channeled through crystals or stones. It's a steady, always-available source of energy and can cleanse and recharge an aura very well, with the benefit of grounding you at the same time. In fact, it's very difficult to access earth energy if you aren't grounded.

Yielding Like Water

As you might expect, water energy is very fluid, but the force it can carry varies with the source to which you're connecting. Rain energy is going to feel different from that of an ocean wave or a rushing river, which in turn will feel different than that of a quiet lake. If you want to utilize the element of water, it is a good idea to take the time to become aware of which type you are best suited to connect to, and pay attention to its vibrational effect on your energy body.

For example, a still lake may provide a grounding influence and access to deep connection with the Earth via life-giving water, which may in turn open you to a feeling of communion with your deepest self. Crashing waves, on the other hand, may provide an energy that feels anything but grounded, yet fills you with a sense of power and vitality. Conversely, you may find waves to be soothing rather than stimulating, while a still lake might make you feel restless rather than soothed and grounded. Different people can react quite differently to the same elements. When learning how your particular energy field interacts with any element, it is often best to start off slowly, taking the energy in small doses, easily grounded if you discover that it doesn't work for you.

Water energy such as that of rain is often most easily drawn by opening and surrendering to it, letting it soak your aura the same way it soaks the ground. As its energy is fluid and yielding, it can change form as needed. Fighting it or forcing it isn't useful, but feeling and opening to water's natural fluidity can help you absorb the energy in whatever way you most need.

Rain in particular can be very calming for a couple of reasons; regardless of where the water came from, its natural tendency is to flow downward into the earth. Following rain's energy can help you ground yourself when you're otherwise having trouble doing so. The rain can also cleanse your aura of accumulated stress or negative energies at the same time.

When you don't have access to rain, you can often tap water energy from other sources such as running streams or rivers, provided they are in a steady state and not a chaotic state such as a flood. A still lake can provide a stabilizing, calming and cleansing influence as we've already discussed, depending on your affinity for it, while ocean energy, with the ebb and flow of the waves, can give you a natural rhythm for your breath while providing a background soundtrack as a focus for meditation.

A helpful thing to remember in working with water energy in whatever form is to allow your own energy to flow along with the element, yielding when necessary, using that fluidity to help yourself release stuck energies and surrender to incoming cleansing energy from Source.

Active Air Energy

The properties of air can vary. In the case of still air, you are acting upon it when you draw it into your lungs or into your auric field, and it is thus a more passive energy. But when air takes the form of wind, it becomes vitally active and often quite forceful. Gusting wind tends not to have a steady rhythm, which makes it more unpredictable and harder to synch with your breath. A gentle breeze is generally easier to work with, but unless it's quite steady, it can still arrive in gusts and the intensity will vary.

One way to take in active air energy is to speed up your vibration to match, riding the energy currents like a kite in a breeze. In some respects, it is akin to water with an ebb and flow, and it can be very cleansing to your aura when you find yourself cluttered with stubborn negative energies that are difficult to let go. The quickening effect of wind can sometimes give you just that little extra push to cleanse yourself of something you'd otherwise have a hard time releasing.

Wind can also help give you an easy boost when you're depleted. It carries enough of its own force that utilizing it is often just as simple as stepping into a gust and letting it cleanse your aura, while at the same time it refills your flagging energy reserves.

It may help to envision your shields as porous collectors, ready to catch and absorb the energy in each fresh breeze. Just make sure that you pay attention to how your energy field is reacting to what you're taking in, so that you don't allow yourself to become overwhelmed by it.

When you feel refreshed and energized, you can simply envision your shields and filters going back to the way you normally keep them. Always remember to ground any excess air energy. You may find it helpful to envision it being released and grounded as you exhale, as breathing is the simplest and most basic way we incorporate this element into or release it from our energy fields.

Better Than Caffeine

One morning, the alarm clock forcibly awakened me, an occurrence that always startles me and makes me want to dig myself a hole, then pull the hole in after me. I hadn't slept enough hours, my mattress was uncomfortable, and I was tired and achy. I lay in bed moaning and groaning, not wanting to get up, hating morning, the alarm clock, and being awake in general. Then all of a sudden, Niall got tired of my whining.

Me: Ahhh, I don't want to get up! Everything hurts.

Niall: *That's enough, beloved. You are a powerful, cosmic being. Ground and center right now, and we'll take care of this.*

Me: What?

Niall: *Ground. Now.*

I felt like a soldier getting a pep talk, except that my drill sergeant truly cared about my well-being, and even his stern admonishment wasn't so stern that I couldn't feel the underlying thread of amusement in it. As soon as I grounded, he led me through a meditation that didn't really have words, per se, but which involved absorbing a lot more earth energy in a different manner than I was used to doing it. It worked amazingly well, filling up my energy reserves and taking away the aches and pains completely.

I asked him to give me the meditation again later, in words, because it worked so well for getting me going in the morning. I knew I'd want to use it again, and I thought others might want to try it as well.

A Brief Preamble:

As with all things, you must first relax. Early morning or whenever you first wake from sleep is often the best time to do this, before outside concerns must come to the fore. Be aware that even if you are on a schedule, your perception of this experience can occupy a much longer space of time than your clock indicates. You have experienced clock time passing much faster than your perceptual experience of it, and this is the same principle in reverse. Instead of what you perceive as minutes being several clock hours, in this instance, what you perceive as a longer time interval can actually take place in just a few minutes. All you need do is set the intention for how you will experience it before you begin your meditation.

If you are afraid you will spend too long and make yourself late in getting up, you can move the meditation to a different time of day or set a secondary alarm. I will say here, however, that an alarm may well undo all the good you did with the meditation, if you find alarms to be particularly jarring to your consciousness. Just use the meditation whenever it fits best into your daily life; you will know when that is.

AWAKENING

The Wake-Up Meditation:

Envision your body, and allow your consciousness to sink into the earth, as if you are lying on top of it and you begin to sink into it as it softens to receive you. Open the root chakra to earth energy, but also imagine that your entire energy field is a network of tiny feeder roots like those on a plant, spreading into the soil beneath you. All of those tiny roots softly and gently take in earth energy the way a plant takes in water from the soil. You do not have to pull hard at the energy; it seeps into you through all of those tiny roots, and you can lie there quietly and allow it to happen.

Regulate your breathing, slow it to match the pulse of the earth, and be as a child held in its mother's arms as the energy begins to strengthen you, replenish you and fill you up with the nourishment you need to survive. Take as much time as you need to allow this to happen; this is a near-passive energy intake in the sense that you do not have to work hard at it, but you should remain mindful of what is happening.

Clear your thoughts of anything other than the feeling of comfort and healing that should come as the energy begins to replenish your stores, heal any aches and pains or shock from waking, and shore you up for your coming day. You will feel your body respond and your energy levels rise accordingly. Remain here as long as you feel you need to, until you feel rested and strong, alert and ready to face oncoming tasks.

Rionagh's note: With this softer, less aggressive energy draw, you will probably not feel as though you have taken in too much, but if this does happen, just keep what you need and release any excess back into the earth. You are already grounded, so this will be simple to do, and you should find it easy to sense your energetic balance point—the point at which you have neither too much energy, nor too little.

Music as Energy

Niall: *The concept of using music in energy work is complex, but we can begin to examine some of the basics here. First, a bit of background. You think of sound as a wavelength, a vibratory signal that can be transmitted from one source and then picked up by a receiver some distance away. Just as sight is not wholly a function of the eyes, but of the giving and receiving of signals on several other levels, sound and hearing follow similar principles. The physical ear receives and transmits the signals, but it is sensitive to only certain wavelengths, and thus limited in its potential.*

You often feel a sound before you hear it with your ears. You feel its vibration in your body, something that even those whose ears do not function properly can feel. You also feel it on an energetic level, due to a connection being made—a resonance between the source and the receiver.

When two beings interact in this manner and the waveforms of thoughts are exchanged, we have the experience of telepathic communication. Our communication, for example, comes through on a different level than the physical, and though you "hear" me in your mind, you do not hear me with your ears. In fact, for this your ears are useless, as due to the difference in our vibratory rates at present, they could not detect my speech even if I were to speak aloud to you.

What we have in our telepathic communication is an exchange of information carried on wavelengths at a deep energetic level. It requires a certain matching of frequencies, in which I attune mine to yours so that you can perceive my thought, but the exchange also requires an adjustment on your part as well. If I lower the frequency of my thought and you raise yours, you are able to pick up the communication.

If you consider that your energy field is vibrating at a certain frequency, then you realize that you tend to perceive and interact with things and beings that are vibrating at a similar frequency to yours. Just as with another being, when you perceive a waveform on any level, your energy field reacts to the vibration. The two vibrations—yours and that of the waveform—meet and either mingle or are repulsed upon encountering one another.

If you encounter a being whose vibratory rate is significantly dissonant from yours, you will either fail to perceive that being at all, or you will feel decidedly uncomfortable in that being's presence. So it is with musical forms and energies as well. Some musical waveforms have an adverse effect on those whose energy fields they impact. Conversely, other waveforms provide not only a soothing effect on a person's psyche and a pleasant sound to the ear, but they also act on one's energy field and can go so far as to change its vibratory rate.

This effect can be particularly efficacious in healing, in which a person whose energy field is damaged or vibrating at a detrimental frequency can in fact be helped or even healed by the application of the proper harmonious waveforms. Consider the function of a tuning fork, and you will understand this principle.

You have read in Celtic lore of the suantraí, the goltraí, and the geantraí—the three modes or strains of harp music used to evoke healing sleep, sorrow, or joy. Again, this goes beyond surface-level perceptions. The effect is so profound because it does not merely reach one's ears and logical mind; it also acts upon one's energy field and realigns it with one of the three states to which we have just referred.

Music can have as much of an effect upon a person as a hypnotic suggestion can, and in fact, that is precisely the effect it has in some cases. If you play music to lift or soothe your spirit, you are using the waveforms of the music upon your energy field every bit as much as you are using the beat, tune or words to act suggestively upon your subconscious mind.

If you would put this to the test, try playing a cheerful or soothing piece of music while driving in rush-hour traffic, and see what effect it has on your ability to react in a more peaceful manner to the frustrations that you encounter. We do not recommend the reverse—that of driving with a loud, demanding beat and aggressive lyrics playing while you negotiate your way through traffic.

You asked about using music in energy work. In order to use this energy in your healing and other workings, you must first develop a greater sensitivity to the waveforms and vibrations produced by the music. We will turn this into exercises that build one upon the other.

Exercise 1

To begin, select music of different varieties and genres. Sit in a quiet, distraction-free place and play each selection one by one. Try to listen to each piece without judgment or preconceived notions of what you will feel. Be aware of what each piece makes you feel. Make note of what reactions it produces in your emotions, in your body, and in your energy field. You may wish to write these impressions down so that you may refer to them later. Did the piece of music raise your energy or lower it? After listening, did you feel depressed or soothed, excited or optimistic? Give yourself an honest evaluation of how you felt, not how you thought you should feel. Your experiences and answers may surprise you.

On a daily basis, you react to far more stimuli than you realize, and it comes at you from all sides. Far too often, music is reduced to nothing more than a background noise, and while you are hearing it and it is having an effect upon you, you may not even be consciously aware of it. Knowing to what you react and in what ways you react will make a difference in your understanding of how you are feeling and why.

Building upon that, you will gain a better understanding of how music and waveforms interact with your energy field and how they affect you on a subconscious level. Understanding this is key to being able to use the energy inherent in musical forms. If you do not know how it acts upon you, you will not be able to interact with it, draw upon it, or use it effectively.

Allow yourself a reasonable period to explore your own unique interaction with musical energy, and do not rush through the exercise. Interacting with each particular genre or type of music over a period of several days, or even longer, would be very beneficial to your understanding and experience.

Exercise 2

In the previous exercise, you explored the reaction of your personal energy field to various types of music, and should have a good idea by now of which ones raise your energy and which ones lower it, as well as the emotional states associated with each type. When you have determined to what types of music you are best attuned, choose a variety of pieces that tend to stimulate you and raise your energy level in a positive manner.

As you listen to these selections, pay attention to your body and to your energy centers. Where do you tend to process the energy of this music? You may notice a variety of physical sensations, such as a tingling in your scalp or in your spinal column that changes with the rise and fall of the notes, or a tendency to tense or release muscles across your shoulders or even your diaphragm in response to the volume, tone, or beat of the music. The way in which you process musical energy may vary slightly from person to person, so it is important to explore and learn to recognize your personal mechanisms for this.

Becoming aware of physical sensations that accompany your processing of musical energy will give you clues to which of your energy centers tend to respond to which beats or tones. It is through these chakras that you will interact with and direct the flow of energy, so it is important that you learn to recognize which chakra corresponds with which type of music (for you). Be aware that while there will be some similarities in your *reactions to the various types of music and even some energy centers which will readily interact with more than one type, each particular waveform/tone/beat has a primary energy center with which it resonates most strongly.*

When you have experienced this exercise with stimulating/exciting music, try it with soothing and calming music, and note through which energy centers you process these waveforms. Knowing where your energetic and bodily awareness taps into the various musical waveforms will be useful in learning how to use the energy for different purposes. Also remember that there are no right or wrong answers here; this exercise, as with all of the other exercises, is a subjective experience, though the underlying principles remain the same.

Exercise 3

Once you have determined which types of musical energy you resonate with most strongly, it is an easy matter to open yourself to the energy and begin to absorb it through your auric field. Note that your shields must be receptive to this kind of energy, so it is important to set this intention at the outset of the exercise if you are heavily shielded.

As the energy waveforms enter through your aura, they are processed by the energy center/chakra that most resonates with the particular music you are using. Pay attention to the sensation of this happening, allow the energy to flow through your chakra or chakras and disperse throughout your core energy layer.

If a type of musical energy you encounter affects you in an adverse way, envision it being filtered out of your aura and grounded into earth, just as you would do with any other type of energy that did not resonate well with your own. Here is where personal responsibility comes into play; you can become aware of and balance, process or ground any energy you take on, if you are paying attention to how it affects you.

Musical energy can be a "quick fix" for a person whose energy is flagging, or at times it can simply be a pleasant addition to one's usual energy source. However, as it is not earth energy, it is considered ungrounded or free floating energy, and thus once you have taken in what you need from the music of your choice, you must still ground any excess and envision the rest dispersing evenly through your aura, so that it does not leave you feeling spacey and ungrounded. Also note that certain types of musical energy can have a similar effect to that of sugar or caffeine, producing a quick burst of energy which, if left ungrounded and not evenly incorporated into your auric field, can fall flat very quickly as well.

Take note of how you feel after you have finished the exercise. Do you feel energized, yet balanced? Do you feel peaceful, calm, relaxed? Did aches or pains in your body lesson or dissipate? You may feel any of these, or a combination thereof. As you grow more familiar with the experience of deliberately utilizing and processing musical energy, you will be able to fine-tune the process (no pun intended) to achieve specific results.

This process is much like the way in which digestion of food allows the distribution of nutrients into your physical body. This is why it is as important to be aware of how various types of energies and waveforms affect your energy body as it is to be aware of how different foods affect your physical body. You will generally want to use the types of musical energy that make you feel strong, balanced, and at peace.

Do not worry if you have the feeling that more than one chakra is involved in the energy intake; often two chakras will work concurrently. For example, a higher chakra such as the brow chakra or the crown chakra may be processing the energy in tandem with whichever of the other chakras most strongly resonates with the music in question. This is especially true of music used in healing work, often processed through the heart chakra and the crown or brow, thus bringing through energy at *high vibrations, particularly when the person using it is well attuned and energetically balanced.*

Naturally, since the different chakras respond and resonate to different music and tones, this makes it possible to use music to heal and energize the individual chakras, should you have one out of balance. It is a good idea to become familiar with your chakra system as well as with the previous exercises, in order to better understand the process by which you will be taking in and utilizing the energy.

Regular practice, including simple meditative exercises, can help develop your skills at sensing and working with various types of energies. The same is true of energy work done in cooperation with a partner. If you wish to work effectively with other beings, whether Sidhe, human or otherwise, then it is vital to get to know your own energy—its nuances, how it responds to your emotions, physical state, or outside influences, and what it takes for you to maintain it in a healthy state. Just as you'd want to maintain a healthy physical body, you also want to maintain a healthy energy body. Regular cleansing and recharging can make a huge difference to the quality and potential of your interactions with others, in all areas of your life.

CHAPTER THREE

HEALING FROM WITHIN

A full discourse on healing is well beyond the scope of this book, and other very good books are available that deal exclusively with the subject of faery healing. What I've included here are some of my personal experiences in being healed by the Sidhe, and also a few instructions they've given me directly in healing technique. Much of this information also pertains directly to the energy work detailed in the previous chapter.

Just Relax

Since I was fourteen, I've had ongoing trouble with my neck and shoulders. I went to a chiropractor on and off for years until I finally had enough income to get adjustments more often. The first X-ray taken of my spine showed that the vertebrae from shoulder level to the base of my skull were almost in a straight line with no noticeable curve. This brought on miserable headaches, which I called "neck headaches" because while my head hurt, it mostly radiated from my neck through the base of the skull upward toward the temples.

I was advised to do exercises to strengthen the neck muscles, and to take calcium supplements, neither of which I managed to do on a regular enough basis to help my cause. When I remembered to take it, the calcium helped somewhat, but the vertebrae continued to go out of place within days of being adjusted. After several years of seeing the chiropractor on a bimonthly or monthly basis, I was convinced that this would never change, and resigned myself to permanent neck problems and frequent chiropractic care for the rest of my life.

After Niall began working directly with me in April of 2008, one of the first things he did was show me how very tense I'd been for so many years. He began by telling me to consciously relax the areas of my body where I carried tension, reminding me often whenever I tensed without realizing it. Sometimes the instructions were almost a litany in my mind, mostly consisting of the word relax, accompanied by small tingling jolts of energy to the muscles or tendons in question. This would often cause them to release suddenly, when I hadn't even known they were still tight.

I hadn't realized just how much tension I carried constantly in my upper body. Apparently, this was one of the ways in which I internalized all the stress of my daily life. I shudder now to think of how many years I went around holding myself rigid against my own fear, worry and frustration. It wasn't until the muscles released their tight hold that I was able to recognize the difference between tension and its opposite.

Giving me a whole new perspective on what "relaxed" actually meant, Niall instructed me in how to stretch out the tense muscles. It involved none of the exercises or standard stretches that I'd ever been shown before. In my mind, I heard and saw instructions such as "lean this way," "let your head drop forward", "pull this shoulder back," or "move your head this way while still stretching your neck." At this point, I didn't question; I just did whatever he asked.

During one of these sessions, I felt another of those small jolts of energy, felt another level of tension leave my body, and then several vertebrae in my neck suddenly popped back into place. To some, this may not sound remarkable, but to me, it was extraordinary. Extreme relief and awe swept through me; in all my life, my neck had never popped spontaneously, without chiropractic intervention. I had sometimes been able to get a few vertebrae to move by twisting my head with my hands, similarly to the way my chiropractor did it, though less effective. But never before had any amount of stretching on my own resulted in my vertebrae moving into place rather than out.

This experience became a daily routine. The first few sessions took place at bedtime and ended in my collapsing into sleep, but as we continued to work on it, I found I was able to bring about this level of relaxation anywhere I was, at any time of day. With a few moments' concentration on relaxing the muscles, combined with the stretching and specific movements, the vertebrae often popped obligingly into place.

At first when I did this, I felt a trickle of energy flow into me as Niall encouraged muscles to relax or vertebrae to move, but before long I began to sense that it was taking less intervention, and I needed less coaching. I also required less chiropractic care.

A few months later, I slept in the wrong position and popped something out of place, lower in my back. The subluxation was in a part of my spine where stretching and moving couldn't fix it, so I went in to see the chiropractor. As she always did, she checked my neck to see if it needed attention as well. To her surprise, she found nothing wrong with it. I'd been treated for neck problems for twenty-eight years, and this was the first time my chiropractor hadn't had to adjust my neck.

I am rather chagrined to think of how much time Niall had to spend teaching me the simple expedient of learning how to relax properly. I'm still learning. I sometimes find myself forgetting and tensing without realizing it, only to remember suddenly (or be reminded) and have to release the tension consciously. But I am getting better at it.

It is amazing to think that this trouble of nearly thirty years' duration was largely undone in just a few months. It makes me wonder how many levels of harm we modern people do to ourselves with our internalizing of tension, our tight schedules, and a plethora of other things that all take their toll on our bodies. We often don't sleep right, eat right, or even breathe right, and we usually don't realize it. We get into habits—many of them subconscious—that we continue for years and have no notion of what we're doing to our health and our well-being. I was just as oblivious to some of this until Niall changed my perceptions with the simple request, "just relax."

Sight

Journal Entry, August 19, 2008

Tonight Niall and I worked a little more on the use of energy to change physical reality, in this case my eyesight. Since we began this work a few months ago, I have noticed that the closer to an alpha state I am, the more clearly I can see things at a distance. I am typing this now without my glasses on, and I can almost see it clearly—it is just a little blurry from my position about two feet from the screen. I normally have trouble seeing clearly from more than about nine inches away from something. I am going to let Niall dictate what he told me about vision:

You think that vision is solely a physical device. It is not. Vision is a matter of focusing your awareness on something in order to bring it closer to you. Thus, when you focus on an object, you are actually moving your attention outside yourself and closer to that object, effectively bringing it within your perceptive reach. Your eyes are merely the tools you use to receive and transmit the images your consciousness brings to you, as though the eyes were an interpreter for the brain, and not the other way around. In this way, you process information into a language or form that you can understand. How you see something is not necessarily the way it truly appears, but your brain must put it into some kind of familiar perspective so that you can attempt to understand it.

Notice how you are able to see things at greater distances when you relax and enter a partial alpha state, as you call it. This is because vision does not begin in the eye, but in another place or state entirely. In this altered state of consciousness, you perceive things you normally would not be able to. Try entering a meditative state, draw up energy from the earth, and then use it to focus on the object you want to see clearly. Make sure that in doing so, you do not lose your relaxed state; tensing up is counterproductive. When you try too hard, you generally fail, just as when you try to pull up earth energy forcibly from the ground, you find it more difficult.

As we have discussed before, you can try to bend things to your will, or you can relax into the flow of energy between you and them. If you try the latter method, you will see a noticeable difference both in the way you relate to things and in the manner in which you perceive them. You cannot force your eyes to change shape or to focus on the back of your retina. You can gently guide them and encourage them to do so, working with the energy to achieve what you want.

In the case of most humans, this will happen slowly, as they are not used to using energy in this way. Most of them are accustomed to bending things to their will for rapid results, using physical or mental force. However, working with energy is not a matter of bending other things to your will, but of bringing yourself into conformity and flow with other things.

If people were to bring their own bodies and spirits into alignment, they would experience the ability to improve their health, change their appearance (that which you've heard of as glamour), or even change their physical forms, as in shapeshifting. But as you have learned with simply changing the focus of your eyes, this is not something that can be learned in a short time. Until one learns how to work within the flow of energy instead of outside it, true physical change is gradual at best. It cannot be rushed.

As I mentioned in an earlier section, since that instruction, the prescription for my eyeglasses did indeed change; it is now a bit weaker than the previous one. Physically, the improvement was not dramatic, just as I was told it wouldn't be, but it gave me an inkling of what could be possible with continued effort.

Garbage In, Garbage Within

When Niall began actively teaching and working with me, he brought several of my bad eating habits to my attention. One of those, I have previously referred to—my addiction to carbonated beverages. During the time from April to September of 2008, I tried to cut down on my intake of cola. His reminders helped, but so did his suggestion of drinking green tea instead. During the summer months, I drank it iced as well as hot. Fortunately for me, I'd already given up sugar in my tea a few years prior, so unsweetened iced tea quickly became my answer to the craving for soft drinks. It wasn't as hard as breaking an addiction to nicotine, I imagine, but it was difficult enough because I'd been a cola drinker since my childhood.

I remember passing the soft drink aisle in a grocery store one day and feeling an instant craving for cola. It was a hot day and I could taste the beverage just by thinking about it. As I forced myself to leave the soft drink aisle behind, I'll admit I was whining a little in my head.

Smoothly, Niall's voice came into my mind, laced with amusement: You're all right, beloved. It made me laugh; because of course, he was right. I could certainly live without that soft drink, and live healthier, at that. The humor helped get me over the momentary hitch in my resolve, though there were many similar instances over that summer. In the fall, I took the final step and gave up carbonated beverages altogether. But the next humorous incident took place much later, when I attended a friend's birthday party.

My friend is highly intuitive as well, and has heard stray comments from Niall on more than one occasion. As I walked into the party, she greeted me with a hug and an offer of something to drink. "What do you want? We have wine and beer, milk, water...cola?" As soon as the last word left her mouth, her eyebrows rose and her lips pressed together. Grinning, she said, "I just heard, 'Don't...you...dare!'" We both laughed, and I opted for water.

Another habit I have is that of not eating enough. I often forget to eat for hours on end. I have nothing against eating; I just forget to do it. And when I've been pressed for time, I have often made a habit of eating junk food and fast food, because that was easiest.

I know what my bad habits are, and I've heard plenty of advice touted by health care professionals. It's just that in our society, we are frequently seduced by the quick fix, the easiest choice, the one that takes the least time and effort. Although information on how food affects our health is out there already, many of us tend to ignore it as though it doesn't apply to us. In fact, we often continue to act as though it doesn't apply to us until we develop a physical problem that forces us to change our ways. Niall gave me the following comments:

You must pay attention to what you eat and drink, and what you use to fuel the machine of your body. We have had many other discussions of this, the main point being that if you put junk food in, junk is all you will have to run on, and it will affect your health on all levels of your being. Another thing to consider is that your choice of whether or not to eat healthily is a reflection of your emotional and spiritual attitudes as well.

Take enough time to care adequately for your body, so the union of spirit, emotion and physicality is a harmonious one. If one area is off kilter, it will affect the others, so it is important to do everything you can to maintain a healthy balance in all three areas. Becoming ill is a sign of imbalance in one or more of these areas.

This is why many have experienced such profound physical improvement when they sought out healers who were skilled in rebalancing the subtle energies, and—this is important—when they fully allowed themselves to know on the deepest of levels that such rebalancing was going to restore them to health. Health is another form of abundance that many people mistakenly think they don't deserve or cannot achieve.

Consider the fact that food is energy in a solid form, and your physical being is also energy in a solid form. If you continually take in negative or muddied nonphysical energy from other people or the environment, it affects your personal energy field and eventually, your physical health. Why should this principle be any different for energy you ingest in the form of food? If you think of food as energy instead of as something inanimate, you will begin to see how great an effect it has on your physicality and the manifested energy that you are.

The foods that have the highest vibrations are those which are the freshest, which have been minimally processed, and in the case of animal proteins, those which have lived in clean, healthy environments and been killed quickly and as painlessly as possible. We understand that your physicality often requires an intake of protein and that your vegetables do not always provide this adequately. Many of the creatures with whom you share the earth also require the energies of other animals in order to live. What is most important is that you consume your food with full knowledge of and reverence for its spirit and energy, and that you avoid those foods whose energies were depleted by toxic chemicals or ill treatment that undermines the spirit of the beast or plant in question.

You have heard the stories of humans who consumed "faery" food and pined away afterward because the food of their world no longer satisfied them. In part, this is because if we offer you food, we are offering you energy, and any energy you take in has the potential to change your very being. The energy of the food you consume literally becomes part of you. If you consider this, it can change the way you think of food hereafter. Changing your relationship with food can also change your relationship with yourself, and the effects can be profound.

Health and Self Sabotage

Over the course of our existence, whether through one lifetime or many, people develop habits that are hazardous to our health and well-being. Some of these habits relate to our physical health and some relate to our spiritual health, but all reflect behavior we develop and then find hard to leave behind. Anxiety. Laziness. Addictions. Compulsions. Procrastination. And so on, ad infinitum. It's amazing how many ways we find to distract ourselves from our true purpose—that of soul growth and our journey to wholeness.

Niall and I had a conversation about this one day when I'd successfully used up my ideal writing time by doing other less important things instead. It was typical procrastination, often followed by feelings of guilt and regret over the wasted time. This habit usually led to my staying up far too late at night trying to make up that lost time from the day—a practice that kept my circadian rhythms off kilter and made me unavailable during most normal business hours. In effect, I was still working the night shift, although I'd left my paying night shift job behind years before. As I was about to leave my computer and call this particular afternoon a bust, I felt Niall's energy surround me in the spiritual equivalent of a hug. As he often does, he deftly turned the ensuing conversation into a lesson:

Niall: *Why do you set yourself up to fail?*

Me: I don't know. But I see that that's true. I do set myself up to fail. I wait until the last minute to start something or finish something, I wait until the odds are against me being successful, and then I make my attempt.

Niall: *This is a form of self-sabotage. If you consistently do this, you will consistently have an excuse when things do not work out as they should. You do this because you do not trust yourself, the process, or the outcome. You need to stop working against yourself. Your intentions are good, but your fear takes the lead. It is because of fear that you practice this sabotage. If it is likely that you will fail given the circumstances you set up, then you will not be surprised when the failure happens. But you must cease this way of thinking—or perhaps we should call it a way of working, because you aren't always thinking clearly when you do this.*

Me: What would you recommend I do instead?

Niall: *Relax. Give yourself the time and the room to work without feeling hemmed in by all the pressures and demands on your time and on your being. Breathe. Feel the moment—every moment. Live in that moment, instead of in the fear of what might be, or the regret of what might have been. All that you need will come to you if you allow it into your being.*

Me: Why do people develop bad habits, anyway? And what do we need to know in order to make changes and leave those habits behind?

Niall: *You remember I once told you that you tend to fall back upon what is familiar to you? Habits form because of familiarity with a certain situation or set of circumstances. They are a learned behavior. Even when the habit is detrimental to one's health or well-being, a person will continue the behavior because they know what to expect as a result. The result may be bad, but it is familiar and therefore a person might consider it better than the as-yet-unknown result of making a change.*

People also form habits out of a need for reassurance or comfort, or out of the need to fill a perceived void in their lives. They perceive that something is missing, but they often do not know what that is. They seek to fill the holes with things, with behaviors or rituals, with people, with food or drink. Deep within, the spirit knows that these things or behaviors will not fix what is wrong or stop the pain. People continue these habits anyway because they do not recognize that those holes within can only be filled with the missing fragments of themselves—parts of their own spirits that they have buried, denied, or given away.

No amount of food or compulsive behavior can compensate for the missing pieces of oneself. Deep healing can only be found within—never without. If you are seeking to stop a hole in your emotions or psyche with something from outside, these attempts give rise to all the behaviors that only make such holes larger, until you literally become riddled with guilt and self-loathing.

In order to get beyond this ineffectual stage, a person with a bad habit has to come to a place of self-recognition and self-acknowledgement. He has to want to change, and that is the part most people find the hardest to effect. They feel helpless in the face of their own lack of power, even if, instead of giving their personal power away to other people, they have given it away to things, substances, or compulsive ego behaviors. This is like allowing a young child to drive your car. The ego is often much less mature than the spirit represented by that ego. This is why it is important to reconnect with your own spirit and begin to act from that place of connection, instead of from the more limited ego/personality.

Given a choice, people will usually choose the path that seems easiest to navigate. Sometimes the most beneficial path is indeed the easiest. But often the path most needed and most beneficial is the hardest path to walk, and requires the closest self-examination and the most honesty. The most frightening thing anyone will ever look upon is one's own darkness, and until he is willing to look into that mirror, he cannot begin any necessary change. Once that inner darkness is faced, however, healing can begin.

Change just for the sake of change is not what you are after. If you wish to implement a change, you do so because you know the result will be beneficial, and you determine that the probable benefit outweighs any stress incurred due to the process. You may also have determined that you cannot continue to function effectively if you continue the detrimental habits into which you have fallen. Because of a sort of spiritual ennui or inertia, you often will not change until circumstances force the issue or until you feel that you no longer have a choice. It is best to take back your own power long before you reach that point. To do this requires an action on your part, an effort of will.

Me: Many people receive advice from Spirit and then are still at a loss as to how to implement that advice. We know we need to make changes, but we don't know how to start the process. It all stretches out in front of us like a daunting task given without step-by-step instructions. Could you give any advice on how to start the process of healing and changing? How does a person begin to make changes happen in his or her life and psyche?

Niall: *It all comes down to living in the moment. If you look at the enormity of the task ahead, you will fail to see the nuances and minutia that make up the process of change. Change is a gradual process, unfolding moment to moment, always. It is ongoing, no matter how long it takes.*

Consider the opening of a flower. You have seen photography that captures this process over a period of time. Hours or days—perhaps even many days—following your first observation, you see the result. If you are not paying attention along the way, like the camera capturing those hundreds of moments of the process of opening, it might seem as if one day, the flower was a closed bud and the next, in full bloom. But each unfolding, each bloom, was made up of many small moments of change which might have seemed infinitesimal at the time, but which continued until the results became quite obvious. Any change you wish to make also begins with one small act. A breath. A decision. A step.

If you cannot think how to make a great change, make a small change that is along the lines of the larger change you desire. If you cannot change your diet all at once, for example, change one small thing about your diet. When you have successfully integrated that change, make another, and so on until you have formed new habits and achieved the result you were seeking. In just such a way are major life changes made.

Living moment to moment does not mean that you do not plan. However, it is a progression; you cannot implement the last part of the plan before the first. When you take that crucial first step, you have already determined whether there will be a result. No result can come from frozen indecision or lack of action. Make changes in your life the same way you would work a puzzle—one piece at a time. If you do this, no change will seem as daunting, and one small change will facilitate another, until the whole thing gains momentum and becomes more than the sum of all those small steps together.

Overlapping

Journal Entry, February 6, 2009

Niall told me that he could show me more of the various ways energy can work, and the ways we can work it together. On this particular night, he had me sit in the dark in the armchair in my office. Then he proceeded to explain why some lore speaks of faeries healing through a human or "faery healer", and a little of how it can be done. He told me to ground myself, and then open my root chakra wider. I asked why, and got the following explanation:

Often when you try to draw earth energy, you try to ground and draw energy through smaller energy points in your feet rather than through the root chakra. Though you are familiar with the concept of grounding through the root, you don't necessarily realize that doing so has several purposes. While this connection does anchor you, it also functions as a conduit for earth energy. Visualize a well, and water rising up through the well. The channel formed by opening and grounding with the root chakra forms the walls and shaft of this well, and when you then open up to the energy, it rises through the channel and flows up, into, and through you. Yes, this is a very sensual imagery, but it is also the most functional way of drawing a large amount of earth energy. You relax, give the energy a place to go, and it flows upward like the water in a well.

Then he told me to open the energy centers at my crown, my brow, and my heart.

Through the crown chakra, our energies connect. This is the seat of our spiritual connection to each other, and when we open and join these chakras, I can then send energy through you to accomplish a purpose. This is why you must open this chakra to me during a healing—yours or someone else's.

When you open your brow chakra, we have an easier time communicating mind to mind. You must learn to filter out the other things that you receive when you open this chakra; you must make the connection selective so that you hear me more clearly and do not allow the other things you perceive to intrude and cause a distraction—noise and mental clutter.

By opening the heart chakra, you are better able to connect with those you are attempting to heal. By this vector, you perceive their energy and can sense what is wrong or needs to be healed in them.

When you open to me fully, I can align my energy with yours so that we overlap, like so.

At this point, it felt as though he were wrapped around me where I sat. I could feel his energy surrounding me—not as though he'd put himself inside my skin, but rather as though he and I were simply sitting in the same space at the same time, our energies connected and overlapping each other. When he told me to open the root chakra and allow earth energy to rise through the "well," I could feel the energy rise through both of us, the two things happening in tandem. It was as though every move I made, he made at the same time, so if I raised my arm, his arms made the same motion, as though we were glued together.

The energy that rose through the well flowed right through my body to about chest level and out through my arms, and my hands and fingers started to itch and tingle with it. Because I was beginning to experience the early symptoms of a cold, Niall had me send the energy into my throat and nasal passages, my sinuses, and my eyes. When I moved my hands, I could nearly feel his arms and hands covering mine. I can't say that it felt exactly like another pair of physical hands on top of mine, because there wasn't any extra weight, but it also didn't feel like my hands alone.

When the exercise was over, he instructed me to ground the excess energy and not to stand up too quickly.

The tingling in my hands did not dissipate until I grounded the energy. The other warning was helpful, too; if you retain that much energy and then stand up too quickly, it can make you lightheaded.

Since this instruction, I have had occasion to use this method at various times in healing work, and my experience has been that when I open to the energy properly, my own energy doesn't become depleted. At these times, I usually feel him just behind me, so close that it feels as though if I leaned backward, he'd be a solid presence there. The healing energy flows through me rather than from me, and I become the conduit for it. I don't even have to worry about directing it—that just seems to happen automatically.

Down Time

During the early spring of 2009, I often stayed up late working on things I hadn't been able to finish during the day. I also kept a hectic daily schedule, and could often be found running here or there on errands for the kids or myself. I hadn't been eating as healthily as I could have. I was often tired and energetically depleted, and spent very little time caring for myself properly. For months, I had either been very lucky, or the Sidhe had generously helped prevent me from catching minor illnesses. They had certainly been instrumental in making my meager hours of sleep benefit me more than would have been the case otherwise.

Then one of my children brought home a virus that seemed to be nothing more than another bad cold. The kids recovered relatively quickly, and even though my husband also caught the virus, he seemed to recover quickly as well. By the time they had all mostly recovered, I had not yet shown any symptoms, so I gratefully assumed that I had escaped again.

Escape, however, was not to be. In the space of a few hours, I developed cold symptoms, and once the head cold had begun to subside, the trouble moved to my throat and bronchial tubes. I spent a week in bed, forced to rest whether I wanted to or not. I'd sleep for hours, awaken briefly to eat or shower, then collapse into bed again and repeat the process. One week extended into two. It soon became apparent that this was not just any virus, but a viral bronchitis with a wracking cough. All told, between the initial illness symptoms and then the subsequent pain from displaced ribs and sore muscles due to all the coughing, I was effectively out of commission for three weeks.

When I asked Niall why he and my other spirit guides hadn't healed me of this illness, too, he told me calmly, You would not take time to rest, and you would not listen. This way, you have no choice.

I realized that he was right. I'd been acting as though I was invulnerable to illness, and had neglected my health in the process. I suppose that as long as nothing happened to take me down a notch, my bad habits would have continued. The Sidhe had simply stopped enabling me to ignore my health and get away with it.

In the hours and days I spent abed, I read many books I might not have made time for otherwise. In the process, I experienced many spiritual epiphanies and jaw-dropping moments as I internalized what I read and what the process revealed to me about myself. What I had most needed was to simply stop and listen. It's a pity that it took an illness to get me to pay attention, but I certainly learned a lot in those three weeks.

As this intensive learning experience progressed, I felt a deeper calm than I'd ever held before. I left my sickbed changed—a more serene version of the person I had been, less prone to impatience and doubt, and surer of my place in the world. Somehow, all the rushing and hectic life events I'd been embroiled in before just seemed so much less important. It felt as though while my lungs and ribs went through illness and injury to healing, my spirit relearned what it was to take a deep breath and simply allow myself to be, with no particular agenda. Now, even when I find myself in the midst of life's habitual chaos, I can take a breath and find that stillness within, no longer elusive, unreachable, or forgotten.

Healing with Stones

Niall has helped me heal, and taught me directly how to use stones in healing. When we worked on a friend of mine in her hospital room after an orthopedic surgery, Niall stood just behind me while I did what I have always instinctively done. I ran a hand over my friend's energy field, feeling for cold or hot spots, and wherever I found them, I pulled the disruptive energy out of her aura with my hand, then grounded it directly into the earth. After I'd used this method to unblock things, the hot or cold spots had either receded or were gone altogether.

Prior to the hospital visit, I'd obtained a chunk of raw blue Apatite at a gem shop because it is believed to help with bone and joint issues and help ground change into the physical body. At the store before purchasing it, I had mentally asked it whether it was willing to help me in the healing of my friend, and I felt a sense of acceptance. At the hospital, Niall told me to take this stone and ask it again for its help in healing my friend. Hearing/sensing its affirmation, I was told to pull up Earth energy and direct it through the stone to the surgical wound. When I did this, I felt a pulse of energy, nearly palpable, from the stone. My friend reacted in surprise when the tension in her muscles and tendons suddenly released all at once.

This healing technique was an amalgam of how I've always instinctively worked healing energy and instructions from Niall, who stood just behind me and coached me through working with the stone.

During my bout with bronchitis, a Sidhe healer showed me how to use another of the healing stones that had come my way. This particular stone was rather unusual; it had petrified root wrapped around the original rock, which made it look veined and organ-like. Worn smooth and shaped by water, it fit in my hand as though it were a handgrip sized just for me. It was an indirect inheritance—I had discovered it in a box of items passed on to me from my husband's late mother. In addition to its other qualities, it had a tiny natural hole through it, though not one easy to look through. During the bronchitis, I felt an impulse to get this stone and try to use it to help heal myself, though it had never occurred to me before to use it for healing.

In channeling earth energy through the stone, I found that rather than pumping energy into my body, the stone seemed to have a drawing action instead. I held it near my damaged ribs and felt it draw away some of the pain and soreness. Had I not been ill and injured, I might not have discovered this property of the stone.

Being Amethyst

I'd been reading Tarot often over the course of one summer, during which I was frequently exposed to many different energies at healing fairs and gatherings. For the most part, I'd always managed to stay clear and not pick up chaotic energy from others, but occasionally I found myself experiencing symptoms that I later found out were indicative of energetic overload.

On one of these occasions, I also needed healing for some tired muscles and out-of-place vertebrae, and could feel indications of partially pinched nerves. I wanted to clear my chakras and aura, and I'd been reading about the healing properties of various crystals. I knew that Amethyst was considered to be a powerful healer, and had some limited experience of its effects. I decided to put some of the Sidhe's healing instructions into practice by asking for help from an Amethyst crystal. I had several small ones, both tumbled and raw, but I'd also recently acquired a much larger piece—a beautiful arch of Amethyst geode. I'd been searching for something like it for years, but pieces of that quality and size were always far out of my price range. This one's appearance in my life had been sudden, unexpected, and astonishingly inexpensive when it should have been prohibitively so. Noticing it sitting nearby, I decided to ask for its help.

I lay down on my bed and placed the Amethyst on the pillow, close to my head. Then I asked it if it would help me cleanse and heal myself. As I lay in the darkness, I took myself through the process of relaxing and releasing my tension. In moments, I began to feel waves of energy pulsing from the Amethyst into my head and through my body.

A tingling began at my head and continued down to my feet, and along with the waves of energy, I also began to see purple. Everything behind my closed eyelids was purple, and it seemed as though I lay inside a glowing purple energy field. Inside that field, I sensed multiple points of crystal, and then I began to feel myself as one of those points, joined to all the other points by a network of energy grids.

In one instant of clarity, I suddenly was part of the Amethyst, just as each tiny point was connected to and part of all the others. I realized that the crystal was not at all motionless, ponderous or slow, as one might imagine it to be. All my previous ideas of what a stone or a crystal was flew right out the window as I felt myself/Amethyst teeming with life and awareness.

I realized that it was neither slow nor quiescent, but instead hummed with an immense amount of energy. The piece of it that lay next to my head was but one part of a powerful, sentient, ancient being. I could feel its awareness of my realization even as it continued to work on my aura and send healing energy though me.

It was perhaps my perception of the Amethyst's awareness of me that reminded me that I, too, was an individual. As I became aware of my human body again, I was overcome with awe and appreciation for the ancient being that had shared itself so generously with me. Tears rolled down my face, and as I got up and put the Amethyst back where it usually sat, I was acutely aware that my perception of it had undergone a permanent change. I had experienced what it felt like to be linked with and part of an Amethyst, if only for a moment.

CHAPTER FOUR

LIFE LESSONS

Life here in the physical realm has never been particularly easy, and each new decade seems to bring its own unique challenges. Since the development of the modern world, we've made many advances in science and technology, and indeed some of those things have made our lives easier, but some have had exactly the opposite effect. In many ways, life has never been more complicated. Priorities might continue to be survival-based, but in the more developed countries they have taken on a different focus than that of our ancestors—all centered on getting what we need and somehow managing to thrive in this modern, tech-centric jungle with its increasingly complicated lifestyles.

With so many society-based processes and issues demanding our time and energy, many people have become harried, stressed, and distracted. The abundance of daily input often includes very little that is helpful or healing. Most of what we take in comes in the form of opinions from outside ourselves—opinions which shape our perceptions of ourselves and alter our behavior and reactions in order to allow us to conform to the current trends of our culture and the expectations of others.

It is no wonder that many people are struggling with emotions and issues based in conflict with others, with self, and with the environment in which we are expected to live and work. As a society, we need to learn some basic skills that will enable us to deal with the bombardment of stressors that come at us daily from all sides. Oftentimes, it comes down to clear communication, patience, and open-minded thinking, all of which are vital tools for spiritual navigation in a very physical world.

Anger Management

How many of us struggle with anger? How many times in a day do we become irritated with someone or something? I used to have a hot temper, but that has mellowed over the years to the point where it takes much more to set me off than it used to. That having been said, there are days...well, most of us know about those sorts of days, when nothing seems to go right. The path to peace and tranquility isn't always an easy one, and it requires that we give up many of our former paradigms, including the way we think about and experience anger.

Journal Entry, November 30, 2008

When I spent some time trying to connect with Niall, I found that I was not grounded properly. In fact, I was very ungrounded. I tried to ground, but I was having a hard enough time that Niall grabbed hold of me mentally, pulled my energy downward, and had me visualize a place underground beneath some big old tree roots. He had me grab onto the roots, then pull earth energy from the roots and from the same place the roots were getting their energy. Finally, I started to feel more stable. I had to really work at it, and for a while I was even sort of dizzy and had a loud ringing in my ears. I always have some ringing in my ears, but this time it was *loud*.

Niall: *You are familiar with the concept of getting more of what you focus on. You have been absorbing negativity from around you, and it was affecting your mood and ability to ground. When you focus on negativity and pour your energy into it, it feeds off you. The more energy you put into a negative direction, the more energy it pulls from you, until eventually you have no energy left with which to function and heal yourself.*

Conversely, the more energy you put into something positive, the more energy channels back to you, so that it actually feeds you and sustains you. If you take time every day to make certain that you are properly grounded and focused on the positive things you mean to effect in the world, you will never arrive at the place where you are being drained by negative energy. It is when you become ungrounded and unfocused that negativity begins to seep in.

Journal Entry, April 2, 2009

This communication came after I had lost my temper and immediately regretted it. I wanted more information on anger and how to deal with it.

Niall: *It is not that the Sidhe do not experience anger. We do. But we have learned to contain it and then to transmute it so that it can do no harm.*

When something angers you, you must first address yourself, and then from a place of renewed calm, address the source or cause of your anger. Emotions are but a reaction to stimuli. You choose how you will react. The stimulus remains the same either way. Remember that you may not be able to change the stimuli, but the one thing you can change is yourself.

This may seem a simple thing, an obvious thing, but it can be surprisingly difficult. Yet you may accomplish it, with practice. When your first response to a surge of anger is to acknowledge the feeling and then reach for the deepest calm within yourself rather than lashing out at others, you will have accomplished the first goal in controlling anger.

Journal Entry, April 6, 2009

I had been experiencing some irritation with a certain situation on this day, and had come to recognize that my frustration was unnecessary and would do nothing other than upset me. Niall was right before about the stimulus remaining the same either way. The situation that irritated me on this particular day would not have changed regardless of how I reacted, but had I reacted with patience rather than the opposite, at least I would have experienced less stress.

I spoke to Niall about how I had been trying to change my reactions to situations I perceived as negative, but how I had not had much luck, as my first impulse still tended toward irritation rather than calm. I was disappointed in myself because I was not reacting as the advanced being I wanted to become. First, I was frustrated by the initial situation, and then compounded things by being frustrated that I was frustrated.

Me: Every time I think I'm doing things right and finally getting an idea of how I should be, every time I start to imagine I might be advancing, I fall right back into the same old ideas, reactions and patterns of behavior.

Niall: *That's because it is what you are used to. It is what you've done for most of this lifetime, and you are acting on what is familiar to you. Everywhere you turn, you are given advice that says to do what is familiar. To "write what you know," for example.*

Me: That's a good point. Can you expound on this a little?

Niall: *Of course. The more you attune yourself to harmony and wholeness, the more familiar it will become to you, until you reach a point where the impulse toward harmony overrides the disharmony you have been taught. This gives way to a deeper knowing, one that will permeate the whole of your being. Peace and the impulse to react from a positive rather than a negative standpoint will become as automatic to you as breathing.*

The dance analogy you are thinking of is a good one. Your teacher has told you that what you practice is what you will automatically perform when put to the test. As you continue to recognize and curb your impulse toward a negative reaction to a stimulus or to an individual, you gradually change your inner conditioning and that of your brain as well. As with your identity and credentials, these reactions are also stories that you tell yourself, a programmed response. Change the program. It is that simple. You create your own reality.

Every part of your being is designed to react in ways that will create the reality that you most desire. If your desire is for a greater understanding of self and the ability to react with calm and serenity rather than with fear-based anger or irritation, then that which is within you [i.e. your subconscious] will strive to create the new reality.

This is why affirmations (when coupled with belief) produce results. They speak to the part of the human brain and psyche that writes the code for how you will think and react. You have heard of the power of the spoken word. Over time and used with intent, these affirmations have a powerful effect on the part of your consciousness that brings about change. If you tell yourself something often enough, you start to believe it, so be careful what you tell yourself.

Journal Entry, October 19, 2009

Me: How can I change my perception so that I don't just look at the negative side of things? How can I get rid of feelings of stress or dissatisfaction with circumstances that I can't control? If I'm miserable, I'd rather not feel that way, so I need to know how to change those feelings, especially when I'm in a situation that I can't change.

Niall: *To begin, you should consider the true origin of the feelings. Remember that your paradigms are made up of bits and pieces of other people's paradigms, which you have fitted together to fashion a belief system for yourself. When you took your current form and created your current circumstances, you agreed to a certain set of rules and modes of living. But who created those rules? Who created the circumstances in which you now find yourself?*

Me: I did? Other people did? Or it was a collaboration that I allowed?

Niall: *Precisely—all of those. By choosing to be born at a certain time, in a certain place, and to certain people, you are in some way setting up what your beliefs will be. The challenge is in moving beyond those beliefs and realizing that all of them were a choice. When one choice no longer serves, you are then free to create something different.*

We have already spoken about how a person may perceive any given situation in one way, while another person may perceive that same situation in a completely different way. What may be irritating to you could be enjoyable to someone else.

When you consider where your perceptions originated, you should remember that the way you think and react is the result of your experiences and the paradigms and beliefs that you chose to accept and integrate.

Children usually either fear or hope that they will become just like their parents, and for good reason. These are the first examples you see of how to act or react. Throughout your life, you experience many other such examples. But you must remember that whether or not you choose to make those examples part of your being and part of your set of paradigms is entirely up to you. You are the one ultimately responsible for your own mode of being, no matter who served as your exemplar. An example is information only, and what you choose to do with it is up to you.

Perception—at least at the mental level—is an amalgamation of paradigms. If you do not like how you are perceiving a situation, you must change the paradigms you bring to it. Let us say that you perceive a certain situation as irritating. Is it really? Why? In order for it to be an irritation to you, you require a certain set of beliefs about it, or about how it "should" be. What if you changed those beliefs? What if you chose to view it differently—if you allowed it room to simply be, rather than automatically categorizing it and judging it?

If people were to realize that the way they feel about circumstances or events is based in choice, they would realize that the power to change those same feelings is also based in choice. Thus, instead of viewing an event as entirely negative, such as a tragedy, instead a person might see that same event as a way of experiencing growth. The ending of one thing always heralds the beginning of something else.

You will not always be able to change your outer circumstances immediately; you may have taken a seriously flawed physical form or given your power or authority away to others, perhaps even at the moment of your birth.

You all lend authority temporarily to your parents, until the time you can take it back again, when you mature. But, assuming you are of sound mind, the one thing you always have control over is the way in which you perceive the people and events in your lives. If you can approach these without judgment, you have control over your feelings about them. When you reserve judgment and allow beings and events to unfold in their own way, your own feelings about them stay in a state of balance.

In order for you to become angered about someone or something, it requires a judgment from you. The moment you place judgment, you have determined how you will feel and what your reactions will be. The longer you can withhold that judgment, the longer you can set aside paradigm, belief and expectation, the longer you remain in control of your emotions, and the less you feel that persons or events are beyond your control. For it is not people or events you need to control; it is yourself.

The only thing or being over which you truly have control is yourself. And in the gaining of that self-control, you should begin to find that your experiences are vastly different. You do not have to be stressed, irritated, angry, or fearful. The events and circumstances of your life, no matter how intense, do not have the power to make you that way. Only you have that power over yourself. Your perception, created from all your learned paradigms and beliefs, is the key to whether your state of being is one of peace or one of unrest.

Sometimes a lesson must be repeated in many different ways and at different times before it really sinks in. Anger in particular is a difficult emotion to deal with, because so often we have no good outlet for what we feel, and we find it coming out in all sorts of different ways. An outburst of anger is frequently due to the fact that we tend to bottle it up inside us while trying to be socially or politically correct. Unfortunately, the longer we bottle up toxic emotions, the higher the toll they take on our health and well-being, and often we don't even realize where all that pent-up energy is going.

Journal Entry, January 6, 2010

On this day, I found myself in a bad mood following an irritating phone call. Later, I was dismayed to learn about some communication difficulties between two people I cared about, and it made me feel worried and depressed. These feelings were enough to staunch my creativity and keep me from writing my fiction, and in thinking about it I recognized that my productivity was always less if I'd had bad news or something was worrying me.

When I realized that I had again allowed relatively small things to put me into a negative mood, I asked Niall to tell me what I could do about it. Despite how helpful his prior communications had been, I felt in need of an even clearer starting point for actively changing my own moods and perceptions, in getting myself out of a bad mood. I might not be able to prevent the initial emotional reactions I had to the various stimuli, but after I recognized and acknowledged that something was bothering me, I wanted to be able to change the bad feelings into something a lot more peaceful and less painful. I needed a very basic, first-step approach to fixing my mood.

His answer probably shouldn't have surprised me, given all our work over nearly two years' time. He told me, *The first thing you have to do is relax.*

I smiled ruefully; this had to be one of thousands of times he'd told me to relax, and apparently, I still needed the reminder. He went on to explain:

Nearly everything you want to accomplish must begin with relaxing, whether it's an orgasm or a simple change of mood. Few people fully comprehend the extent of the link between one's energy and mental/emotional state and the physical body. The state of one can change and affect the state of the other, most profoundly.

When you are in a bad mood, take a few moments to pay attention to what your body is doing. Are you tensing muscles? A clenched hand or jaw, a tightening of the abdominal muscles or a rigid spine—any of these or similar are outward signs of the unease you are feeling emotionally. Unfortunately, rather than moving the energy out of the body, these tensed muscles lock the energy in and hold it.

You cannot truly let go your anger, frustration, worry or any other sort of negative emotion unless and until you relax the muscles that your body is using to hold onto the energy. If you can find the areas of tension in your body and actively relax them, you should feel an immediate sense of relief emotionally. Once relaxed, you will find it much easier to change your negative perceptions to a more positive focus.

He was right; I had indeed tensed several muscles in reaction to my stress. I then had to make a conscious effort to recognize the trigger points and release them. When I took just those few moments to release most of the tension hoarded in my muscles, I found my bad mood altering at once. What's more, even my breathing changed as my diaphragm relaxed and my lungs filled more easily.

As I sat there breathing, I came to realize that during the course of my lifetime, I had often gone around in a state of emotional and bodily tension without knowing it. Apparently, I did it so often it had become habit, and even though that particular habit had eased considerably in the time I'd been working with the Sidhe, all too often I fell back into those old familiar and ingrained modes of being.

If we could simply master the art of recognizing our own tension signals and giving ourselves a much-needed, conscious break from that tension, we would all probably live longer. We would certainly live happier.

Stressing Out

Originally a night owl and a night-shift worker, I'd never really gotten back onto a more typical daytime schedule. Instead, I'd kept to my habit of staying up very late at night, ostensibly working at my computer while making no useful progress on my writing. I often spent the time doing mindless things that didn't require me to think too hard or feel too much. If I considered what I was doing at all, I thought it was an escape from the things that stressed me out in my everyday life, but as Niall explained to me, I wasn't really escaping anything.

One night I'd just wasted a stretch of several hours in front of the computer and had no measurable progress to show for it. All I'd accomplished was to tire myself out and give myself a headache. Nevertheless, I felt guilty for not getting anything done, so I pulled myself together, grounded, centered, and prepared to channel—or so I thought. And I did get a response from Niall, but it wasn't what I expected. Instead, it was exactly what I needed.

Niall: *Don't you realize what you are doing? Your habit of staying up until nearly dawn is a stress reaction. You feel stress concerning your daily life and your finances, and so you punish yourself by staying up late and* *refusing to care for yourself adequately. And yet, you get nothing done! You are not alleviating the problems that cause your stress; you are contributing to them. And now you want me to aid you in this endeavor, so you will feel less guilty for not getting any work done during reasonable hours.*

Go to bed. I mean it. I will give you the information you seek, gladly, when you have rested and when you have resolved to work during more equitable hours. I cannot be a party to you abusing your body.

Me: But night is a good time for me to do this. It's quiet now.

Niall: *It was quiet four hours ago, also. Please go to bed. I love you.*

What could I say to that? He was right. This incident was just another of his timely interventions, meant to help me get myself out of a detrimental habit that wasn't serving my highest good. But it started me thinking about stress itself, and the many ways in which we tend to damage ourselves with it.

Stress is one of the leading causes of death in our busy modern world. Although it is not tangible and we may not smoke it or eat it, we may smoke or overeat because of it, and we internalize it regardless. Stress takes a horrible toll on our bodies and our minds. Perhaps the most insidious thing about it is that we often don't even realize we're having a stress reaction at all, because we've gotten so used to the discomfort that we don't pay attention to the warning signals our bodies are giving us.

This became very clear to me one day when I stood before the window of a district health office, going through the red tape required to get my children some immunization boosters. I was more anxious about these boosters than my children themselves were, and my mind was also full of all the other things I was responsible for, that day and beyond.

As I waited for the receptionist to finish what she was doing, I felt Niall's energy come up behind me, and heard him whisper the one word he has probably said to me more often than any other: *Relax.*

I realized suddenly that my shoulders were tensed and raised, and I wasn't taking full, proper breaths. As soon as I realized this, I dropped my shoulders and drew in a breath the correct way, starting from below the diaphragm rather than the chest, instinctively grounding as I did so.

Instantly, I felt my energy settle, dropping into the floor beneath me and spreading outward, anchoring me. The relief it brought became obvious to me at once. It amazed me how much difference just one small change of mindset and posture made in my ability to wait patiently, support my children through their immunizations, regain and retain the calm I should have been walking in but had somehow left behind when I departed from my home earlier.

Given that anxiety and stress is so very common, I was eager to glean any further tips the Sidhe might have on how to deal with it on a daily, regular basis. Naturally, it was in the course of another typical busy day that some of the information I needed flowed through, relevant as always to the situation at hand.

On this particular day, I was sitting at my computer, mentally in work mode, and Niall wanted me to take a moment to center myself before I started working. He wanted to address my feeling of pressure to get work done, and my sense of guilt when I don't.

Niall: *Just relax, love. Breathe. You do not always have to be working.*

Me: But I feel a pressure to get things done. I feel that time in which I'm not getting things done is time I'm wasting.

Niall: *How do you know the time is wasted? The time you take to center yourself, to breathe and allow yourself to be, is not wasted. If you never take time for this, then you fall right back into the trap of time itself, with all its illusions. How do you feel in this moment? Balanced, centered, whole? Do you feel that there is nothing you have to do or be, no expectations placed upon you? How rare a state is this? Do you see how valuable this is? How then, can that be wasted time? Just be with me. Stop thinking.*

There. In this moment, we can live one of your lifetimes. In this moment, we are timeless. Did you feel it? Did it have meaning to you? Then it was not wasted. Each moment, just as each breath, is of value. You must not count yourself so cheaply that you feel unworthy of such value. You are worth every breath; you are worth every moment. Do not begrudge yourself this.

All the moments you spend in learning this are of value also. In a very important sense, they are also a part of the work about which you are so concerned. If you do not do this, then the rest of the work is of no consequence. It will all have been for nothing. If you would not waste all of your hard work, then permit yourself to have these moments of stillness, and many of them. They are what all the work leads toward and springs from. Do you see?

Me: Yes.

Niall: *Good.*

Guilt vs. Remorse

Me: Could you say something about feelings of guilt, and how one might deal with those?

Niall: *Guilt is a perfect example of a reaction based on your acceptance of the paradigms of others. It is one thing to feel remorse when you make a foolish mistake or act in a way that harms another—especially if you* *acted out of anger or a callous disregard for the sanctity of another. Remorse is meant to keep beings from repeating the same mistakes—it can be a useful learning tool. But guilt is actually a different emotion from remorse.*

Guilt is the result of the amalgamation of paradigms that we spoke of before. Often when a person feels guilt, it is not because he has done something truly evil, but because his set of beliefs—and thus, his actions and reactions—opposed or caused inconvenience to someone else's set of beliefs. The emotion of guilt often springs from a lack of confidence in oneself and one's own "rightness." As often happens, you may have taken a completely benign and valid course of action, but because your action collided with someone else's perceptions and that person reacted badly, you then bash yourself mentally for what you did. You then begin to perceive yourself as wrong or flawed, when in truth there is nothing wrong with you other than the fact that you are now punishing yourself for not having the same set of paradigms as the person with whom you had the conflict.

Ask yourself this: must there always be a right and a wrong? Cannot there be two rights or even two equal wrongs? Who makes these determinations?

This is where judgment comes into play—again. When you carry guilt for perfectly valid ways of being and acting, you are judging yourself, and usually not by your own standards. A chronic carrier of guilt has judged himself by someone else's standards, and found himself wanting. Those who constantly fail to forgive themselves or others for either real or imagined shortcomings have usually accumulated a set of beliefs and standards that even the most advanced of beings would find difficult to embody. And the worst of it is that rather than providing guidelines leading toward a higher state of being, these standards and judgments usually goad one into a very limited state of being.

Your best method for dealing with guilt is to learn to recognize when it stems from judgments that come from outside your being. Guilt always stems from judgments, regardless, but those that originate in someone else's perceptions and not your own are particularly crippling, because in accepting them, you have given your power away to another. In order to release guilt, you will have to release the judgments that created it. This can be difficult, as people tend to hang onto their most limiting paradigms, but once you do release them, your whole being will feel lighter.

I had never considered before that stress or even guilt were choices, having always viewed stressful situations and the anxiety that accompanied them as things beyond my control. Just becoming aware that I could choose how to perceive potentially negative events and circumstances made a huge impact on me. As a result, my perception began to alter to fit this new reality.

Forgiveness and Obligation

Niall: *It is vital that people learn what forgiveness truly is. Forgiveness, like love, should be unconditional, and once given, should not be taken back. In its way, forgiveness is a similar contract, to be honored and upheld.*

This is not to say that just because you forgive harm or wrongdoing, you must now make yourself available for more harm or wrongdoing at the perpetrator's hands. As in all things, you must exercise wisdom. You can forgive someone who has done you harm and yet still maintain yourself out of harm's way. Neither true forgiveness nor true love is blind to the other person's faults. Forgiveness is not masochism. It is perfectly all right to forgive someone for hitting you, to accept and understand his tendency to throw punches. It is also perfectly all right to step aside from a second blow should you see one coming.

We would also say here that the ability to know when to remove yourself from an untenable situation and when to end an unhealthy association is an important piece of wisdom to cultivate. Many people believe they must wade back into the fray repeatedly because the person with whom they have the conflict is a family member or someone else to whom they have made a commitment. They feel that no matter how bad it gets, they must continue to try to "help" the person in question. Often, this is an obligation that the well-intentioned person has set upon himself, but in some cases, both parties may be better served if the one trying to help releases himself from that perceived obligation.

Sometimes no matter how much love lies between two people, the one simply cannot help the other, and what was intended as help may instead hinder. One person may simply not be capable of hearing necessary truths from the other, and may need to hear those truths put in a different way from a different set of lips. If you find yourself in a situation in which you have tried to help a friend or loved one and this person seems unable to hear you, consider that you may be doing the person a greater service by stepping back from the situation and allowing him room to learn from a different teacher.

This is not to say that you must abandon your friend or loved one, but rather that you trust that person to learn the lessons he needs to learn in his own time and in a way best suited to his needs. Sometimes in the stepping back and releasing of those bonds of perceived obligation, both parties experience greater healing than might otherwise have been possible. In the process, a great weight is lifted from each.

Ultimately, no person can be entirely responsible for another. The responsibility for the learning of each lifetime rests with the soul living that lifetime. It is not an obligation that one can shoulder in another's place. In short, no matter how much you may wish to help, you cannot learn your loved one's lesson for him; that is his responsibility and his privilege alone.

If, as sometimes happens, a relationship or association must end in a parting of ways, it is important to release judgments you have made even as you release the relationship. If you carry judgments about the other person along with you even after you have parted, you are still carrying the energy of all your negative interactions with that person, and it will weigh you down even after he or she is supposedly gone from your life.

Forgiveness requires more than just speaking the words, however well-intentioned they may be. Forgiveness means that you lay down your judgments about the situation and release the energy of the interaction so that true healing can occur. This makes it possible to move forward without the bitterness, without the pain and the sense of loss.

In the time since Niall first gave me the above information on forgiveness, I've come to understand it much more fully than I did at the time, though as always on any spiritual journey, there is always further to go.

I think that when many people contemplate forgiving someone else, they only get just so far. This happens for various reasons, which may include the misconception that forgiveness equals condoning the other person's bad behavior.

Insincerity also plays a part. A good example of this would be the people who, on their deathbeds, suddenly ask forgiveness for all the negative things they did in their lifetimes. The likelihood that all of these people are experiencing true remorse seems slim.

All too often, it is fear of consequences—Hell, or an unknown afterlife—that finally inspires some people to confess and ask forgiveness. If they were not on their deathbeds, they would most likely get up the next day and go back to living their lives exactly the same way they'd lived them all along. Is it any wonder that some people have a hard time forgiving those whose "sorry" might be nothing more than lip service, if indeed they gave an apology at all?

An insincere "sorry" and an equally insincere "I forgive you," such as might occur between two children whose parents are forcing them to reconcile after a fight, are both equally false. So forgiveness cannot be mere lip service and a vague intent. It must be genuine if it is to bring about true healing, whether for the person being forgiven or the person doing the forgiving. Only then does the energy of the situation actually change.

How, then, do we even begin to forgive when the anger or hurt is still so potent? A possible answer lies in the way we think about forgiveness.

The important thing to remember here is that forgiveness isn't about whether the other person is truly sorry, or whether or not they have been adequately punished for their bad behavior. They may never be sorry and they may never be punished within our current lifetimes. That's just a fact of existence, and we have to accept it if we are to ever be free from it. Some bullies, criminals, and people with nasty, cruel tendencies are going to get away with their bad behavior for a while, and maybe a long while. Maybe it will even be more than one lifetime's worth of getting away with it.

In the meantime, we who may be dealing with those individuals in the present need to remember that it might not be our particular job to bring them that karma, mete out that justice or pass that judgment. It might be someone else's job to do that, and it most often is.

So, given that it's usually not our job to punish those who wronged us, and given that vengeance is usually a bad idea, what purpose does it serve for us to keep holding onto our pain, anger or hate over what they did to us? When we hang onto anger and hurt, we aren't punishing the person who wronged us or meting out any kind of justice. Instead, we are punishing ourselves, endlessly.

Further, when we hold onto hurt and anger over another person's words or actions, we are very effectively continuing to give that person our power. Why in the world would we want to do that? All the negative emotion directed at the other person translates into a stream or tendril of our personal power attached to that person and that situation.

Unforgiveness = Attachment. Whatever we cannot let go of tends to hold us prisoner, and based on witnessing the effects of bitterness taking root in people's lives, I truly think the state of unforgiveness and the harboring of anger and resentment is a very slow form of energetic poison.

The act of forgiveness, on the other hand, is actually very closely related to the act of detachment, and detachment from a negative energy, person or situation equates to taking back one's personal power. That very act gives one a sense of expansive, joyous freedom.

It is important to understand that by forgiving someone you are not condoning their bad behavior, and your forgiveness does not render them unaccountable, in terms of karma, for what they did. If they have not learned from the situation with you, they will still have to learn that lesson from another situation, another teacher, later on in their soul's development. Don't worry; they won't get out of the lesson forever--not if they want to advance. You can let someone else be their teacher. And believe me, they will encounter that teacher, in the proper place, at the proper time. In the meantime, you deserve the freedom that forgiveness can give you.

Now on to some initial practical application. Just how does one start this whole forgiveness thing? Remember the equation: Unforgiveness = Attachment. So the first step is to locate the energetic cords that you have inadvertently attached to the person or situation and begin to cut those cords.

You can ask for assistance; there are higher-level beings out there (angels, spirit guides, or whatever we might call them) who are very good at helping with this sort of thing. A high-level elder among the Sidhe or a healer such as Airmid or Brigit might also be willing to help, if you've cultivated a cooperative relationship with them. But the truth is that you can also just sever any attachments yourself.

You can either envision a flaming sword or something similar, and cut the energetic cord you've attached to the negative person, or you can just envision the cord untangling from them and drawing back into yourself. If it's a cord they made, cut it and let it snap right back at them, no longer tethered to you.

Envision that you leave all of their energy behind with them, and just take back whatever energy you have given to that person or situation. Every time you get angry about what they did or feel angst over the hurt they caused, you are giving them more energy, so your task is to stop the leakage. Take back your energy and learn to stop sending it to them.

Once you have it back, you will probably have to cleanse and transmute it thoroughly, but there are all sorts of ways to do that. You can envision your returned energy being bathed in white light, passing under a silvery rain, or any other cleansing visualization that works for you, and keep up the process until you feel that it has been fully cleansed and reintegrated. When the process is finished, you should feel a sense of peace regarding the situation and the now-resolved energy entanglement.

After you have cut the energetic cords between you and the person who wronged you, you will gradually begin to feel more objective about the situation, since you are no longer pumping energy into it. With that objectivity will gradually come a greater understanding about where the other person is on their soul's journey, and with what limitations they might be dealing.

Again, this doesn't excuse what they did, but it should at least begin to explain it, and that insight will further distance you from the emotion of it, so you can finally let it go.

In time, you'll begin to look at people as other souls on a similar journey to yours, just at different stages of that journey. It is okay for them to be wherever they are, just as it is okay for you to be where you are on your path. Every student learns at a different and individual pace; that's part of how this "3D as classroom" system works.

Gradually, this understanding translates into a feeling of expansion and freedom on your part, as you learn how your energy feels without attachments to the negative person. The more freedom you gain, the more of this expansion you experience, the easier it will be to open the chakras associated with forgiveness and personal power, the heart chakra and the solar plexus.

All of this eventually leads to complete forgiveness—the part where you can actually feel genuine love for the person despite what they did, despite whatever their current situation might be, and despite their possible tendency to repeat their mistakes. It all starts with the first healthy act of detachment, which begins the healing process and leads to transformation.

Fear

This issue is among the very hardest for most people to face. As you read this, you have no idea how many times I restarted this same paragraph, simply because I wasn't sure what would be the most appropriate way to introduce the subject. Perhaps the most meaningful way would be to say that I've been there, in spades. I've struggled with fear throughout lifetimes, and to be truthful, I still struggle with it. I have never met anyone who hasn't struggled with it in one form or another.

The process of working through fear, panic or even just simple worry was such a frequent occurrence in my life that until I began working on final edits to this book, I'd never really thought to ask Niall for a specific commentary on fear as a subject. However, as the information flowed effortlessly through and we put actual words to concepts he'd been teaching me for the past few years, I was glad I'd finally done so.

Niall: *If you stop and truly examine any negative emotion, you will find that the root cause is fear. In particular, people fear loss, whether that be loss of love, loss of resources, or loss of self.*

Envy, for example, is based in fear--the fear that if someone else has something, there will not be enough left for you, or that it will somehow threaten your position. This is an instance of the fear of loss of resources.

There are many other examples, but suffice it to say that the fear of loss has been a part of the human experience for a very long time. Thus, it is one of the hardest things to come to grips with and rid oneself of. It is this fear that has set one group at odds with another from the very earliest days. It will not be until people can rid themselves of this limiting way of thinking that the human race as a whole will be able to move past this issue.

Me: How can individuals begin to work through fear? It's a hard process, as at each turn, circumstances seem to reinforce the fear.

Niall: *Fear is another emotion that must be worked through in small steps, and it is an ongoing process. Grounding and releasing the energy of fear is an important first step. As when we spoke of your anger, you must recognize the part of your physical body where you are holding the fear, and then take steps to relax that part. Find out which chakra corresponds to the body area in question, and envision the governing chakra as being calm and of proper size, about the circumference of a mid-sized orange. Undertake meditations designed to help heal and balance that chakra. Think about opening yourself to universal energy and abundance, and allow yourself to feel the gratitude associated with that abundance. It is impossible for you to feel fear and gratitude at the same time.*

In order to fully release fear, however, one has to change one's way of thinking. When something goes wrong, often one's first reaction is fear of what the consequences might be. But there is always a lesson to be learned in any set of adverse circumstances. Once you open yourself to recognition of what that lesson is, it becomes somewhat easier to move through the situation without becoming paralyzed by fear of the unknown.

Fear, as with any other type of energy, can be grounded and released into the earth. Find your connection to the earth, and allow the unwanted energy to drain from you. Whenever you find yourself feeling fear or panic, do this, no matter where you are or how often you must do it. Over time, it will become second nature, and you will find yourself releasing and grounding fear almost automatically. A side benefit to this is that your fear or panic reactions will also begin to occur less often.

It is important that you do not judge or criticize yourself for having a fear reaction. Simply note its presence, ground, release the uncomfortable energy, breathe in healing energy from Spirit, and move forward again.

Hearing Spirit Guides and Allies

Niall: *It is important to know that you are not alone. Though you may not see them, each incarnated being has a group of spiritual allies and loved ones on the other side of the veil, fully cognizant of the situation and fully willing to assist and provide support— energetically, mentally and emotionally. No one actually goes through a negative or frightening experience alone, regardless of the perception they may currently entertain.*

Me: I've heard many people say, "I called for help from my guides/allies/angels and I didn't get it. I keep listening but they never answer." What is generally happening there?

Niall: *This sometimes happens because, in their fear, people hold their energy and shields closed against anything that might come at them, and in so doing, they also close themselves off from the energy and support that is readily available. A tightly closed fist is not a hand open to receive.*

The subconscious can only allow so much through at one time, and most often, a person's baser emotions take precedence. If your mind is preoccupied with fear and worry, it leaves little room to allow anything else through. But it is the subconscious pathways that are most easily accessed by those of us who would communicate to you from this side of the veil, so if you would wish to ask advice of us when you are in the midst of a difficulty, it is important that you learn how to ground your fear, relax, and open to the communication.

That having been said, being open to and practicing those connections when you are not in a state of difficulty can help keep the pathways clear and allow direct communication with guides to become familiar to you, so that whenever you need to hear from us, you are able to do so.

Me: In other words, "Don't just call us only when you're in trouble? Stop for a calm chat now and again?"

Niall: *Precisely.*

Me: What about those people who aren't necessarily panicking, but they just feel that, for whatever reason, they can't hear their guides?

Niall: *It all comes down to relaxing and allowing, and also trusting that the information that comes through to you is real.*

All too often, when trying to receive communications from their guides, Sidhe, or other such contacts, people expect to hear a different voice inside their heads, much the way you would expect to hear the voice of another physical person with your ears. They assume that this voice will have some different timbre or tonal quality than that of their own mental voice, but when the guide's words come through in the same way as their own thoughts, people are often confused by this and cannot tell the two apart. It can take time and practice to learn to tell the difference.

For those who experience this sort of confusion, I would advise paying particular attention to those thoughts that seem to arrive suddenly, yet carry good, useful advice or information that pertains to the situation at hand.

Also remember that a guide may or may not always communicate directly in words. Sometimes their language comes across more as symbol or imagery, or a sudden burst of knowing. Pay attention to the small things—the repeated themes or events or images you encounter, the synchronicities that you might otherwise miss if you aren't paying attention.

With time, you will learn to distinguish your guide's typical methods of communication, and you will be able to recognize the feeling of the guide's energy whenever they are attempting to communicate with you.

Maintaining regular contact of this sort can often go a long way toward alleviating the fear and anxiety that comes from the belief that you are alone without help or advice.

Validation

Niall: *Many people feel a need for frequent approval by others. They constantly worry what others are thinking of them or what others will say of them. They desire their actions to be acknowledged, approved of, and thus validated by a source outside themselves. But in this need for such validation, they do not realize that they are giving their personal power away to others—to a loved one, to an acquaintance, to a stranger on the street. Many are the ways in which they seek approval from others, all the while refusing to grant that approval to themselves.*

Where did so many humans get the idea that only actions seen by, agreed with or lauded by others are valid? Your spirit is not subject to approval by one being or another. You do not need others to give you permission for your existence. Yet many of you seek a consensus of approval before you will act, or you seek what you call a "pat on the back" whenever you perform an action, no matter how ordinary it may be. Often, if you do not get this acknowledgment, you become very unhappy, allowing your joy in your creation or action to diminish or disappear altogether.

This is akin to the concept of needing to be thanked for the giving of a gift. If you are a person who is not happy unless the recipient of your gift thanks you or acknowledges you in some way, consider that in your need for the validation of their thanks, you are giving your own power of self-determining approval away to another person. In another respect, you are giving a gift and then expecting payment, which defeats the purpose of the gift in the first place.

If, however, you give your gifts freely, perform your works and actions with confidence and joy without the need for acknowledgement or praise, you are reclaiming and honoring your own power to create, do, or be. You need no acknowledgment other than your own joy in the creating, the doing, the being.

If you are only giving a gift or performing an action so that you will be thanked or validated from outside yourself, not only are you giving a gift with strings attached, but you are also hampering your own ability to create freely. Creative works or even thoughtful acts meant for another's enjoyment are your way of sharing and connecting with all that is around you. Such works and efforts are meant to enhance your way of relating to the world, and to invite others to engage with you in your joy. The joy should come from the work—from the doing and the completion—not from the moment others tell you they find it good also.

This is not to say that you cannot take delight in the appreciation of others, in the shared joy of accomplishments. But be aware of and careful of your own expectations, and know that true approval or disapproval must come from within, not from without. The work itself must be its own reward.

In a universal irony, you will find that when you are at peace with yourself and your actions, when you are no longer desperate for the approval and adulation of others, you release your hold on the energy and allow it to flow freely. It can then flow back to you. With no need, desperation, or judgment attached to the energy, the very approval you once sought will come to you after you no longer require it in order to feel happy and complete.

A very important thing to remember here is that need and desperation combine to create a stranglehold on energy. In your desire and need for validation, you block the flow of power away from yourself and direct it to others instead. But when you realize that you are fine without outside validation, that you can be whole and fulfilled without it, then the energy of joy you put out in your efforts to create for creation's sake will flow back to you through the open, unblocked channel you have made. Such freely flowing energy is boundless, created and re-created repeatedly through your realization that you already are all that you need.

Another important thing to remember is that people do not necessarily quest after validation simply from a need to have their ego stroked. They seek it for all sorts of superficial reasons that stem from a much deeper need, a much deeper reality. The perceived need for validation and acknowledgment comes from the disconnection and separation so many people experience, a fear that they are forgotten or deserted, forced to tread their paths alone and without encouragement. "Can anybody hear me?" becomes a forlorn refrain.

Validation from others seems to reassure them that they are indeed not alone, that someone "out there" cares about them or at least about what they do. They feel that without obvious acknowledgment, they have not made a difference in the world, even if this is far from true, and so they look for reassurance. What they are really seeking, however, is connection, not validation. Once a person rediscovers his connection to All That Is, the need for external acknowledgment lessens because the energy-based support, the love, the feeling of being part of something greater than himself is already present.

When I first realized that it would be good to include some of the Sidhe's thoughts on people's need for validation, I was still working on my own need for it. I hadn't realized the need was so great that for over two decades, it had contributed to my inability to become a published author. I'd lost some of the joy I took in my writing, and even a trip to the bookstore, where so many books sat with other people's names on the spines, could occasion a dark night of the soul. Surely, after so many long years of effort, the tide had to turn in my favor, or so I thought.

As I worked with Niall, I began to experience a shift in my energy and way of thinking. I still desired validation, but whenever I embarked upon an activity meant to let me give without expectation, create without the need for acknowledgement, and engage with the flow of universal energy, I found that gratitude and positive feedback came to me without my having sought it or even thought much about it. It wasn't in the field of fiction writing, either, but in the field of spiritual healing and intuitive work, and the energy it produced was amazing and transformative.

I began to open up to others enough to feel what they felt, and my empathy kicked in to a degree that I had to shield differently so that it didn't overwhelm me. Small but transcendent moments easily moved me to tears, and there were many such moments. I began to live in an underlying state of joy and profound gratitude.

During that time, I channeled much of the work you see in this volume, and also some short stories deeply connected to the Sidhe. In fact, I think connection is the one word most closely associated with the stories—a common theme in all of them. My ego was deep-sixed somewhere along the way and I simply wrote for the joy of writing, the way I used to do as a young person, before dreams of publication distracted and distressed me so much. I still marketed the short stories to magazines and anthologies, but I became much less attached to the outcome. The rejections registered, but much less so than ever before.

Then one day I stumbled upon a particular market that struck a deep chord within me. In the call for submissions, I read the description of the type of story that was wanted, and realized that one of my recently written short stories seemed especially tailored for this venue. When, upon reading the submission guidelines, I found myself literally misty-eyed from a profound feeling of rightness, I knew I had to send the story there. Other venues might pay more, but it wasn't about the money. I knew without a shred of doubt (for once!) that this was where the story belonged. I submitted it for consideration, and—in an unprecedented act for me—let go of my expectations for the outcome.

Nine days later, I received an email asking whether I'd be willing to make a couple of clarification changes to the manuscript and then resubmit it—a rarity in the field of short fiction. I promptly emailed back with an affirmative, made the minor changes required, and sent it back in. A week after that, I received another email, this one informing me that the story had made it through the first reading and would be held for further consideration. Then came a wait of more than two months during which I heard nothing. The final deadline for submissions to the venue came and went. A few days prior to the date specified for final acceptances and rejections, I still hadn't heard anything, and I refused to sit and worry about it. I turned my attention to other things.

Then suddenly an email appeared in my inbox, and after the first six words, I knew. "We are pleased to inform you...."

The neighboring states might have heard my shrieks of delight. Finally, after decades of "no," a publisher was finally telling me "yes." Published at last—it was what I'd been striving for, what I'd always wanted. I was quick to share my good news with the people closest to me, and a few dozen of their friends.

Congratulations poured in, and in a superficial way, I did feel vindicated for all my years of effort. But it wasn't the same experience I had once thought I'd have upon my first publication, because underneath the initial exultation, I felt something else. Deep inside and rising like a wellspring, the emotion that came bubbling to the surface was gratitude. The same profound, misty-eyed gratitude that had sent the story on its way without a guarantee of the outcome. The same gratitude I'd been walking in all during the past year of intuitive work.

I felt more joy in knowing that particular story—a story that only existed because of my connection to things intuitive and because of my connection to the Sidhe—that story would be the first published. The congratulations were nice, but they hadn't brought tears to my eyes, and they hadn't caused the overflow of love I felt in my heart. What made me weep with joy and gratitude was the knowledge that my desire had come about in part because I'd learned how to let go of it. I'd finally begun to get out of my own way and let Spirit flow.

Unlimited Resources

Like many people nowadays, I have often wondered how to meet all the demands put on me by family and society. It seems there are never enough hours in the day in which to accomplish all the things on my list of responsibilities. Consequently, for many years, some things remained undone for months on end, while other things that seemed more important took center stage and used up all my time and energy. I found this extremely frustrating, and the more the various activities crowded my life, the more I felt as though I were unable to do justice to any of them. Perhaps the biggest frustration was one shared by many people, especially those who have families—the feeling that you must always come last on the list, and that your needs are the ones most often relegated to the back burner.

I was in the car running errands when Niall promised to give me more information on the subject. That communication came through the next time I sat down at my computer.

Niall: *One of the reasons people become impatient and angry at one another is because your current society dictates that you spend all your time and resources meeting the needs of others and of society itself. This leaves you very little energy to work with, and many of you reach the end of the day feeling tired and out of sorts.*

Think of your energy, patience and self-control as a well that must be refilled periodically from a much larger aquifer so that it does not run dry. This is another instance in which it all comes down to perception. People think that they cannot take time to care for and recharge themselves. They tell themselves that other things are more important. But this is a fallacy that must be corrected if any individual is to stay in balance.

Without direct access to Spirit, the well of creativity, joy and abundance dries up. Humanity has become a slave to the clock and the calendar. With the pressure of schedules and unmet needs, a sense of martyrdom begins to build. It is far easier for a person to tell himself that he cannot take even a moment to see to his own needs and to blame the neglect on someone or something else than to acknowledge that he was the original creator of his own prohibitive schedule, his own stifling reality. What better to blame than a clock, a calendar, or a schedule? The alternative would be to take responsibility for one's own well-being, but many people have forgotten how to do that, or they believe that circumstances prevent them from doing it.

In truth, few people cannot find even a moment to ground and center their energies at a few or even several points during the day. It takes very little time to do this, and can be accomplished in a quiet moment at a desk or on a quick trip to the water cooler. You lose track of how many breaths you take every day, and yet this is necessary for your very survival.

You would do well to think of taking conscious time to ground and to allow earth energy to replenish your flagging reserves as being easily as important as breathing. If you become accustomed to taking moments of quiet at any opportunity during the day, there will come a point at which your connection to the Earth and to Spirit will be automatic. In one breath, you can take in oxygen and earth energy at the same time. One breath—such a small measure of time and effort for such a profound benefit. And as you need to breathe anyway, not one instant of time is "wasted."

If you never allow your energies to become depleted, you will be far less prone to frustration, anger or exhaustion. If it can be said that you owe anyone anything at all, then you owe it to yourself to make sure your needs are met. You may have noticed that your anger flows more readily when you are tired or have been meeting others' needs consistently without seeing to your own. It is at these times that you will tend to perceive others as unreasonable, stubborn, or argumentative. Your own skewed or jaded perspective dictates your experience at such times, and would often be different if you did not allow yourself to become physically, spiritually or emotionally depleted. And yes, all three of these areas are important.

It does not take longer than a good, focused moment to shore up your spiritual and emotional reserves, so the excuse of never having time is erroneous. Your experience of time is based on your perception of it. In much the same way, your experience of spiritual and emotional abundance is also based on your perception of it. If you perceive these resources as infinite, then that is what you will find them to be.

AWAKENING

This brings us to the last part of this communication: the perception of abundance. You have heard of the adage that some people view a glass as half empty while others view the same glass as half full. The problem the "half empty" group has is that they perceive their spiritual and emotional resources to be finite. They believe that they only have so much energy, time, or patience, and that at some point, these things will reach an end. The principle of abundance is that it has no end. If you instead chose to believe that you had plenty of patience and understanding, you would create this as your new reality. You would cease to believe the fiction that your patience was wearing thin or that you would never be able to understand this or that person. You would stop giving away all your power and resources in this manner and would instead draw power and resources to you.

In the analogy of the glass, what most people do not realize is that the "half full" group also has a problem. Despite their more positive attitude, they still only perceive the glass as half full. Why half full, when it could be completely full? Emotional and spiritual resources are infinite. All you have to do is open to the abundant love and energy inherent in the world around you, and you will fill with those resources, which will never run out. Energy produces energy, love produces love, and so on. You get more of that which you focus on, and if you focus on abundance, that is what you will draw into your life and into your being. If you focus on your resources as being finite, then finite is exactly what they will be. As always, you choose what you will experience.

This principle of infinite resources is tied to the mystery of the sacred well in faery lore. For now, think of the sacred well of abundance or the cauldron of plenty, and realize that these are both conduits through which you may tap into the infinite resources of earth energy and the source of All That Is.

Journal Entry, May 10, 2010 – Resources at Hand

Recently, I was sitting in my car with the engine off, eating lunch while in the middle of running errands on a hectic day. It was early spring and raining, and while I ate my food, the temperature in the car gradually dropped until I was feeling chilly. Turning the engine on and letting it run was out of the question due to fuel prices and environmental concerns, and eating while driving was an option best avoided. I had a light jacket with me and put that on, which helped, but my legs were still chilly.

After a while wherein I sat there getting colder by the minute, Niall quietly pointed out that my winter coat was lying in the passenger seat next to me. If I wanted to be more comfortable, all I had to do was reach out, pick up the coat and use it as a blanket to cover my legs while I finished eating. What was the point of having resources at hand if I was not going to reach out and take them?

He was right, as usual. Such a simple and ready-to-hand solution to a problem, and I hadn't even noticed it right away because I was so accustomed to doing without. I'd spent many years expecting to tough things out on my own, effectively denying myself access to the comfort I needed just by dint of not seeing the resources that were literally right at my fingertips.

I realized that this habit extended to other areas of my life, in which I denied myself the things I needed or wanted out of habit, when often, I could have had them at little to no cost or even any inconvenience to anyone else. If I never reached out for what I needed, who but myself was to blame when resources didn't materialize?

This was what typically happened when I denied myself physical-world resources, but what of the resources of spirit? What of my tendency to deny myself access to my inner world contacts, or to the Well of Abundance that I could easily tap into just by reaching out? What we make a habit of doing is what we tend to fall back on when we're not consciously thinking about it.

I realized that Niall was right; I needed to make a habit of tapping into the infinite resources of the universe, recharging my energies and making sure to see to my own needs, rather than denying myself and trying to trudge ahead on limited spiritual and emotional reserves.

What I had not realized was just how much I'd been denying myself while trying to forge on alone. There was a difference, I realized, between independence and self-denial.

While I cannot claim to have fully internalized these lessons yet, I can say that they have already changed my life for the better. I'm more willing to make sure my needs are met, whether those needs are physical or spiritual. In taking those few moments to replenish my spiritual resources when I need to, I find that the promised energy is there and easily accessible. Now I often find myself taking a deep breath in the middle of a hectic day, on the road in traffic or right in the middle of some demanding task, connecting with earth energy and feeling an immediate sense of peace and well-being flowing into me.

If you've spent a significant amount of time worrying, feeling frustrated or helpless, then the change from those ineffectual emotions to feelings of confidence, peace and power will be even more astonishing when it happens.

Joy

Niall: *Joy and peace are really two facets of the same state of being. Peace is joy in a passive state, while joy is the active expression of peace. Unfortunately, joy is often poorly understood. This is because what many people think of as joy is limited to feelings of exuberance or moments of exultation when something extraordinarily wonderful has happened. Some have lost the ability to register anything but the most extreme of emotions; they find themselves jaded, or oblivious to the myriad sources of joy inherent in every moment. Joy is often found most strongly in the quiet moments, and in the most ordinary of circumstances. A touch or glance from a loved one, a moment of synchronicity, a thousand small connections or affirmations—all of these can comprise a life lived in a state of great joy. Again, perception makes the vital difference in whether a being feels joy or only discontent and lack.*

When people focus on negativity, pain and fear, they tend to forget or ignore smaller moments and events that should lighten their spirits. They then tell themselves that there is no joy in their lives. But joy does not have to be dramatic. Every time you take pleasure in the company of another, every time you breathe in a pleasing scent or appreciate the taste of your food—all of these small, ordinary moments carry the potential for you to feel joy. Joy, peace, contentment...all are related, all are connected. If you can recognize one, the others are there ready to hand.

Joy stems from a sense of rightness and balance—the sense that one's life is functioning as it ought despite any conflict that may be present. Joy can flourish in an environment of uncertainty, but in order for that to happen, you must have access to that innermost knowing, the soul-deep sense that despite any chaos or strife, you remain fully supported, perfectly safe and whole at the deepest levels of Spirit.

Joy springs from the same well of abundance that provides unlimited resources and support. When one taps into Spirit, one taps into the very source of joy. Thus, even when circumstances are trying or less than ideal, when you are strongly connected to Spirit, you can still have an underlying, deep joy that changes the way you experience life in all its facets.

Living in the Modern-Day World

So often nowadays, I see people hurting, unsure of where to turn as our modern world becomes more and more chaotic. I hear similar stories from people from all occupations and lifestyles; they tell me they're overwhelmed, that they don't know how to make a difference, how to find peace for themselves, or how to function in a society that often seems increasingly blind and deaf to Spirit.

Those who do embark upon the path of the seeker and open themselves up to Spirit find their empathy growing, which makes them even more sensitive to all the nuances of energy, all the vibrations of pain and anger around them. Sometimes they feel as though they don't know how to hold or deal with all the emotion welling up. This is understandable; a deeper connection to the Earth and to other beings can bring pain as well as joy. This happens because hearts and minds open and stretch to encompass a much larger reality, and things people were able to ignore in the past can no longer be denied. The damage we've done to ourselves and to the Earth becomes more and more apparent. For some, the pain is so deep that it makes them want to withdraw from society and nurse the hurt, hoping it will go away.

The good news is that the number of psychics and sensitives is growing, but the bad news is that many of them have no idea how to deal with their gifts, and their well-meaning loved ones have no idea how to help them cope. It is amazing that in an age wherein we have so much information available, we still find ourselves in difficulty as we try to separate the wheat from the chaff. Some sources of advice are inconsistent. Some are suspected of being hoaxes propagated by people who just want to make a buck off of other people's need for a belief system to follow. Some are too esoteric, the language so convoluted that the texts are hard for anyone but their writers to understand.

Help and useful advice is out there; the trick is in identifying and locating it, since what is helpful for one person may be next to worthless for another. One person's divine revelation may be another person's hokey bit of garbage. The recognition of Truth is individual to each person, and that's okay. But it doesn't make the search easy or even necessarily universal.

What I'm hearing from friends, Tarot clients and others is that we need better coping strategies. We need to know how to deal with all the bad news, negative energy and increasingly depressing global-scale events bombarding us. Thus, my question:

Me: What advice do you have for those who find themselves struggling to cope with modern life and what we call the "rat race?" How can we experience peace and healing when it often seems that society and our fellow humans are self-destructing around us?

Niall: *Get a glass of water.*

Me: What? I mean, I'm thirsty, but...a glass of water...now?

Niall: *(smiles) Yes. It's an analogy.*

Me: Okay. I'm happy to take care of my thirst, but...go on.

(At this point, I went and got the water. Then he explained.)

Niall: *Your most basic, immediate need was one that you were easily able to fulfill—a small thing over which you had control. In meeting that need, there was one less thing with which you had to concern yourself. This is how it starts. Each need fulfilled, no matter how small, is a step toward peace of mind. As we have mentioned in the section on healing, when you cannot deal with things on a larger scale, you deal with things on a smaller scale and gradually move upward. You deal with life one moment at a time, one issue at a time, one decision at a time.*

Remember, time is not linear, though it appears that way to you. In every moment lies the seed of contentment, of wholeness. It exists as infinite potential. It becomes what you make of it. All lives are lived one moment at a time, until you eventually realize that it is all just one very long moment.

Now, given that you currently experience time as linear, what can you do in this moment? No one thing may immediately change the world or your experience of it, but when you string all those moments together into a lifetime, you may have something extraordinary. Rather than worrying over what will come tomorrow or next week, focus on what is here with you now. What can you do now that will pave your road toward peace and wholeness? What will bring you comfort or solve a problem in this moment?

This is not a matter of focusing on instant gratification and ignoring larger problems, but of gaining a sense of balance and harmony that ranges from a smaller scale to a much larger one. How can human beings make a positive change in the world without first making a positive change within yourselves? Your collective outer reality reflects your collective inner reality. Collective human reality at this time is showing an outward manifestation of excess, devastation and lack of harmony. In order for this to change, you must begin with a manifestation of inward harmony, whereby you begin to heal yourselves and the planet. Then instead of trying to effect change from an inward state of imbalance, you start from a state of balance.

Even as you are a larger organism made up of many tiny cells, so your life is made up of moments that form a much larger composite. No moment is insignificant, unless you make it that way. No moment need be wasted or filled with despair if you instead choose—for that space in time—to focus on hope instead. String those hope-filled moments together, and you will have hours, days, weeks, and so on. In looking back, you will find that hope prevailed not because of any huge, sweeping thing you did, not because of any type of deus ex machina rescue from outside yourselves, but because of all those tiny moments in which you chose hope over despair.

You have heard it said that like attracts like. If you all moved forward with hope from one breath to the next, changing the small things and building upon those until you could change bigger things, joining yourselves in a shared attitude of hope and desire for peace and wholeness, you could change the world.

Me: As within, so without?

Niall: *Yes, that is the general idea.*

Me: How might individuals address the issue of helping to make a larger change in the world, assuming we have the resources to do so?

Niall: *Building on the principle that like attracts like, there are things you might do to help manifest the healing you want for yourselves and the planet. Get involved in activities that raise awareness of the environment and of the need for a direct reconnection of humans with nature. Involve yourselves with like-minded individuals and with groups that are better equipped to take action. Don't withdraw; that is the surest way to hamper any concentrated effort to change things for the better. No one likes feeling helpless; if you take even a small action, you will feel less powerless, less carried by the waves around you.*

Remember what we said about tapping into the well of unlimited resources. This is the time when that principle comes more fully into play.

But this time, instead of merely meeting your own most immediate needs and replenishing your personal reserves, you will be pooling your efforts with those of others to bring about a greater change.

Spend time meditating, centering yourself and bringing your energy into a greater state of balance. From that place of balance, reach out to connect with the Earth herself, facilitating an exchange of energy. Visualize the Earth as whole, even as you visualize yourself as whole. Each draws strength from the other, and this builds exponentially. If enough people do this, it can have a much greater effect than you might realize.

It is the same principle as that of manifesting personal abundance, but now it is put into use in manifesting healing and abundance on a global scale. Spend time each day sending energy toward this goal and replenishing your own energy as well. Even if all you have is a few minutes each day, your intention will begin to have a ripple effect. Your thoughts, your intentions, make a difference. It may not be immediately visible or outwardly evident, but it will set something in motion nonetheless.

Also consider that your own changes, your personal journeys toward integration and wholeness, contribute to this energy. The more people who heed the call of Spirit and move toward their own reintegration, the more energy for change will be unleashed in the world, both in the world of matter and in that of spirit. It is a process, and a partnership. The more you trust the process and your role in the partnership, the more easily change will begin to manifest. By their very energy, those already awakened to a deeper reality will help to wake those who are not.

It will not be the gloom-and-doomsayers who bring about this change for the better. It will be those who use the principle of abundance to manifest change in themselves and in the world around them. Everyone who comes into contact with such energy is affected in some way. Given that your energy is part of the whole and contributes to the whole, it is vital that you determine what attitude and energy you will bring into the mix.

CHAPTER FIVE

EVERYDAY MAGIC

Often, what seems like magic to one person or group is simply a different sort of science or technology to another group. Essentially, that's what we're looking at here. And yet even when you change your way of looking at energy and relating to it, the process that unfolds when you truly utilize those connections holds such wonder that most of us would likely still call it magic.

Magic, at least for me and I suspect for many other people, is a term we use to describe our perception of the numinous. It holds all the dreams we had as children, it holds our sense of wonder, and it speaks to the part of us that remains non-jaded and doesn't want to explain away every wonderful, mysterious or outright miraculous occurrence in bland, scientific terms. We want to know how "magic" works, and we don't—both at the same time. The word conveys a sense of mystery, of something just enough beyond our ken that we behold it with awe.

I asked Niall and the Sidhe to give me some practical information about what people often consider to be magic, since so many people seem to have such differing views of its application, how it actually works, and whether it is all just a re-ordering of the consciousness of the practitioner vs. a more overt manipulation or wielding of energy.

Again, we ended up with a chapter that dovetails into the previous ones. Each topic is really just a different view or aspect of the same basic principles, so the energy workings and techniques that apply in one area directly relate to all of the others.

Connections

Niall: *Perhaps the closest thing to what one would term magic is the process of manifestation—that of aligning energies to bring things to you or to bring desired events into fruition. For the purposes of this communication, let us use the terms "magic" and "manifestation" interchangeably.*

The first thing one should understand is that nothing can travel along a blocked pathway. In order for you to manifest things that you need or set events in motion, a way must be prepared for this to happen. A connection must be made between that which is desired and the one who desires it.

You have heard it said that the shortest distance between two objects is a straight line. So it is with energies; hence the references to the "old straight tracks" in faery lore. If there are no obstacles for which the energy must compensate, a manifestation happens much more smoothly and quickly. This is not to say that obstacles cannot be overcome in time, but sometimes there are gaps to be bridged before something may come into being. Often a greater manifestation comes about through a series of smaller ones, each forging a link in the chain until the distance between the intention and the desired outcome is breached.

There are times when a person may feel that he has focused his will to such an extent that nothing stands in the way of his success, but when whatever he is striving for does not appear, he does not understand why the desired effect did not materialize. He does not realize that he can be his own obstacle, which happens when one harbors unrecognized feelings of ambivalence toward that which he believes he wants. You cannot manifest something if you do not truly want it. Perhaps the hardest thing for some people to do is to be scrupulously honest with themselves. It is far too easy to convince yourself that you want something when in fact the reverse may be true.

Clarity is also a factor in manifestation. If you are confused about what you actually want, what eventually arrives may be muddled and vague, just as your original thought was vague.

It is important that a person learn to listen to his own inner silence. This may sound like an odd concept, but if you consider it, you will begin to understand it. For it is in the deepest silence and stillness of one's own being that magic begins—and it begins in no other place. If you want something to come to you, you must make a place for it and begin to align your energy to it. You cannot manifest something if you feel yourself separated from it. Manifestation is forged from connections, from the principle of like attracting like.

This can be a difficult concept to grasp. Some people feel that there are those to whom everything comes easily, and that those who already have things keep getting more. They feel this is not fair, and constantly wonder whether they will ever get what they want. What they do not understand is that abundance builds upon and attracts abundance, and this always comes from an attitude, a state of completeness within. It cannot come from a feeling of lack, or "have not." If lack and striving are the energies you bring to a manifestation, lack and striving are what you will attract.

This is not to say that a person born to riches is always destined to attract more riches or that a poor person cannot experience abundance. Affluence is not to be confused with abundance. Abundance, or the principle of attraction, is not about what you have. It is about what you are. If you speak to those who experience consistent manifestation of what they need and want, you will find that they rarely worry about how something will come to them; they simply know that it will come.

Once you overcome any feelings of doubt or lack, the process of manifestation is remarkably straightforward. Be clear about what you want. Be open to its arrival and never spend time worrying about it. Instead, take whatever steps might be necessary to set things in motion while cultivating a calm focus on the desired goal. It is important to make a distinction here; calm focus is entirely different from obsession and worry. The energies are different, thus the results are different.

Open yourself to what you want and align your energy with it without trying to force the result; this keeps the path clear for the energies to flow, and allows the process to happen. The more practice you have in doing this, the more natural it will feel, until it becomes second nature.

This is really not such a mystical process, which is why we say that magic and manifestation are in fact the same thing. The alignment of energies and the making of conduits for energies to flow from one place or state to another is paralleled in your science. It is simply another way of accomplishing a result, and has a firm basis in what you might think of as the laws of nature.

Me: Speaking of it not being so mystical, can you say something with regard to those who think magic should be more the way movies portray it? So much of what you tell me sounds just like plain common sense that I'm sure there will be those who won't feel it's mysterious enough.

Niall: *We are sorry if anyone feels disappointed by the lack of wands, flashes of light or special effects. It may not seem as wondrous for something you manifested to arrive in a box delivered to your doorstep rather than to* *materialize out of the air, but we have spoken elsewhere about perception and preconceived notions of how things "ought" to be. Those who desire special effects are thrill-seeking and will end up discontent no matter how much unexplained phenomena actually takes place. These types of people are not after knowledge for the sake of knowledge, but merely desire to be entertained. You already have vast amounts of resources devoted to that.*

Limits and Parameters

Niall: *In the practice of what you term magic, you are told to set specific limits on spells, to carefully define their parameters. This is because a thing undefined is also unlimited in its power and scope. It exists only as vast potential, which can manifest in any form. In spells, which are crafted for a specific purpose, you seek to trap and define part of this potential. Sometimes you wish to limit the manifestation so that it does not have unforeseen consequences. Other times, you want to avoid setting limits, as the very parameters you define might exclude different or even better forms the manifestation might take.*

Now think of your own beliefs about yourself and others. These very beliefs and parameters are in themselves a sort of spell, if you will. You have taken a manifestation and set limits upon it, or upon your perception of it. If you define it a certain way, you will tend not to define or see it any other way, even if your vision does not reflect its true nature. Say, for instance, you perceive someone as stingy or mean-spirited. Is that truly the way that person is, or is it the way you have defined him or her based on limited knowledge? For someone else, that same person may be a revered benefactor. Their experience of the person in question may be completely different from yours. What you believe, what you know, manifests your reality.

Me: Could you talk a bit about the concept of moral limitations concerning magic? For example, I have encountered individuals who wanted to hex people with whom they were in conflict, and I have encountered those who abide stringently by the "harm none" principle. What advice would you give people who practice magic and want to know whether there is a universal law or a thing such as karma that governs magical ethics and morals?

Niall: *Ethics and morals exist solely in the mind of the individual concerned with them, and vary according to the preference of each person. Energy is only energy; it is neither good nor evil. It can be put to whatever purpose an individual desires, if he or she knows how to work with it and within it.*

Also remember that one person may have a different ethic than another, in much the same way that what is perceived as injury or insult to one may be of little consequence to another. So to say that one set of ethics and morals govern magic is like saying that all kingdoms abide by the same laws. Certain laws of nature, such as the ways in which energy works and may be worked with, are relatively universal. But the motives of those who work with it vary according to each individual consciousness.

The best advice we can offer concerning the ethics of your workings with energy comes in the form of a simple reminder. Everything you do has an effect on everything else. We are all tapping into the same vast source of energy. We are like fish all swimming in the same lake. There is really nothing you can do that does not have an effect on the water. Thus it is with your use of energy.

We have spoken before about what happens to the anger/fear energy put out by so many people, and you have seen many examples of people who were able to sense when the energy of a place has retained an uncomfortable or "negative" vibration and echo due to painful or traumatic past events. If you are looking for an example of how to behave with regard to your use of energy and your contribution to the vast sea of energy within which we all live and work, consider what your methods and ways of working will add to that sea on the whole. Eventually, the ripples of what you do will reach someone else.

In short, whenever you do something, consider your connection to the whole, and then decide for yourselves whether your methods or actions will add peace and stability, or whether they will add disharmony. Creation is one large symphony. What will your note be, and what effect will it have on the music, once added to the score?

Notice we do not say, "harm none," because as we have already discussed, some view harm differently than others. It is not so much a question of all beings coming into conformity with all other beings that determines the harmony of the universe. Rather, it is a question of all beings coming into alignment with themselves and recognizing both their individuality and their connection to the All That Is, both at the same time. This is harmony. This is resonance. When each note strikes true, the greater harmony will be restored.

Me: So are you saying that even beings who operate in ways in extreme opposition to others still contribute to the greater harmony, as long as they are being true to their original natures and resonances?

Niall: *Yes, up to a point. The disharmony comes not from being individual, but from being drawn away from a true knowing of oneself. Bear in mind that those who have developed a perception of themselves as somehow superior to others or whose energy is that which most would consider evil have often gone far afield from their original states of being. But consider also that human ideals of morals and ethics do not necessarily govern all other beings.*

We are not advocating homogenization here, but rather that each individual consciousness return to its purest state so that each resonance sounds cleanly and purely. When this returning and re-tuning occurs, it will become apparent just how perfectly each of those notes fits into the greater harmony of the universe. Consider these concepts when deciding on a set of ethics and morals for yourselves in anything you do, whether it is magic, or something you would view as mundane.

Goals and Manifestation

When you want something badly and can't seem to get it no matter how hard you try, it's difficult not to become discouraged. You think you've done all you can to manifest what you want, and then time after time, it fails to come into being. It sounds very noble to be able to set aside all wants and desires and just live in a state of what some call "being-ness," but it is also human nature to set goals and work to attain them. It is human nature to dream, even if some of those dreams are individualized and small when compared with ideals of spiritual or cosmic significance.

Over the past few years, I've been learning a difficult and often surprising lesson on goals, dreams, and the manifestation thereof. Here, then, is a part of that journey; I'm still on it. Maybe I'll see some of you on the road.

Journal Entry, February 28, 2009

We began by talking about goals, and what they are to accomplish. Niall told me the following:

People spend a great deal of their time being anxious about the future. Much of every day is spent rushing toward some goal or outcome. What they do not realize is that instead of rushing toward the goal, they need to bring the goal to them in the present moment. Then they are no longer chasing it; they are attracting it, drawing it to them.

You have heard it said that the journey is the destination. When the goal, the outcome, and the journey become one, all is accomplished and the anxiety that accompanies striving for something is eliminated. Approach each desired outcome as though it is already here with you, in the present. Perform whatever actions are necessary to bring that outcome into your current reality, all the while remaining calm and inwardly still. Know that at each moment, you are doing all that you can to bring about the result you desire, and be content. Be calm in that moment; live fully in that moment. In this moment.

When I sat down to figure out what subjects this book was supposed to cover, I knew there would be a section on manifestation. I wasn't sure what I'd say, since I knew very little about how to do it, even given the above communication. That all changed over the next few months, and it's been quite a ride since.

My former method of manifesting things I needed was to pull out a credit card. But with the economic crisis came a crisis for my human husband's business. A startup business that had almost begun to support us during the summer of 2008 almost went under that autumn. We went from nearly enough income to no income at all, and this continued through most of 2009.

For several years since my husband had been let go from a computer programming job from which he'd hoped to eventually retire, we had been living on the last of our savings and investment money. The investment fund took a hit when the stock market crashed, leaving us with very little of what had once been a decent amount of money.

Naturally, we had to economize in any way possible, which meant cutting out dance classes and other nonessentials, and figuring out how to eat on an extremely tiny budget. We'd been on a local and organic food kick, and tried to buy our food as close to home as possible, with a few exceptions like tea and coffee.

Suddenly, the prospect of buying food at all was a problem, much less buying luxuries.

During the late spring of 2009, a friend gave us some cherries, but the lovely big apricot tree that we'd gleaned fruit from the year before had been removed from its spot in a public area, no doubt for convenience, because someone didn't want to have to clean up the unwanted apricots that used to fall onto the walkway.

My dismay was twofold; a beautiful old tree had been killed, and now my family could not glean the fruit it would have provided. After my initial upset, I reached a state of resigned peace. I sent out a silent request to the universe; my family would like a few more cherries, and we'd like a way to replace those apricots that would have been. I didn't consider where these would come from; nor did I dwell on the possibility that they might not appear.

Only a few days later, my daughter and I were sitting in my car in a parking lot when a car pulled up beside us, bearing friends we'd not seen in at least two years. When the mom of the family asked me how we were doing, I mentioned that we were fine other than the lack of funds. She at once offered me cherries from her tree and apricots from a tree belonging to her neighbor, who never used the fruit and would be glad to have someone come and get it.

Astonishment and delight are the only two words I have for my reaction. Here was exactly what I'd asked for, manifested in such a way that no money needed to change hands, and in a way that otherwise might have seemed like coincidence. I'd simply asked the universe for what I needed and not been attached to the outcome, and it had manifested. But that wasn't the end of it.

My 18th wedding anniversary was coming up that August, and I'd been looking at a new Brazilian restaurant wistfully, thinking that I'd like to try it out one day when I could afford it. Not long afterward, a card appeared in the mail with a special "buy one entrée, get one free" offer—for that very restaurant. My husband and I went out to dinner there and enjoyed it immensely, for half the price. Other similar things began to appear—coupons for free miniature golf, free gift cards from clothing stores, free frozen yogurt.

I'd been thinking that the fruit had been wonderful, but I knew we also needed vegetables, and my small garden spot in the back yard would not grow enough food to feed four people, two of whom were teenagers. Then my friend with the cherries and apricots emailed me to tell me of a community garden near her that was asking for people to come and glean their green beans, of which they had so many that the beans were going to waste on the vine. There is such a thing as a free lunch. Such is the nature of manifestation.

Then there were the dance classes for my daughter. We were told that the group in charge of her dance school might have a scholarship program for people undergoing financial hardship. When we asked about it, we were told she could have her lessons free of charge until the end of the year. Soon thereafter, she revealed that her dance shoes were too tight, and I put some of her old shoes up for sale in the hopes that we'd be able to use the money to buy her a used pair that fit. Otherwise, I didn't worry too much about where we'd get her next pair of shoes.

A short time later, a pair of almost-new shoes the next size up from her old ones were turned in to her dance teacher by a new family who had moved into town. When asked how much money the family wanted for the used pair of shoes, they explained that they never sold shoes back at their old dance school; they turned in the used ones and let them go without charge to anyone who needed them. "Is it okay if we don't charge any money for the shoes?" they asked.

Back in the whip-out-the-credit-card days, I didn't know what abundance really was. I see it now all around me. It seems like magic, but when I reread that initial communication from Niall about attracting things to you rather than chasing after them, I saw that it's really about being clear about what we want and need, and then making an energetic connection between us and whatever it is we wish to manifest. While it often requires some action on our part, it comes without the worry, fear, or anxiety that people usually experience when they develop an attitude of have-not. When we lose the fear and are able to trust that we'll have all we need, things begin to fall into place with much less difficulty.

Manifestation seems to require a blend of action and trust, clear intent and flexibility, and the experience of genuine, soul-deep gratitude rather than a sense of entitlement. With each successful manifestation comes a greater feeling of joy and trust that the universe truly will provide for us. What a blissful experience that is, after so many years of harried, worried striving.

As I went through all of this, I began to realize that the process of manifestation was multifaceted. It wasn't just about getting things, even if some of those things were highly necessary for survival. In fact, manifestation wasn't about survival at all. It was a process of melding spirit with form, both in physical reality and, more importantly, in spiritual reality. The things I'd manifested—food, money, shoes...those were all outward indicators of a much deeper manifestation within my being. In the process of learning how to attract those needed things, experiences, and relationships, I'd become something more than what I'd been when I began, and this new person was a lot less stressed out about life in general.

Bending Time

How many times have we wished we had more time in which to do the things we need to do? It sometimes seems as though there are never enough hours in the day. In today's hectic world, time seems to work against us as often as not. Yet that same experience of time flying past us can also work to our advantage, usually when we are engaged in a diverting experience or a creative work. The phenomenon that writers and artists know as "flow" is one such example.

My own experience of this is that once I engage fully with my writing, time seems to stop. I find myself caught up in the act of creation, unaware of what the clock is doing, so merged with the work that I have no concept of how many hours have gone by until something interrupts my work or my physical body forces me to stop by becoming stiff or hungry. Often, I'll come out of writing flow and find that three or four hours have passed, though I feel as if I've been writing for perhaps a few minutes. But the clock and the number of completed pages indicate otherwise.

I have often wondered how a person might begin to work with time in order to slow it or speed it up deliberately according to one's need. I suspect that with most things, it requires practice and a fundamental alteration of one's paradigms, but from what I've experienced, it is possible to alter time. Niall gave me a very basic explanation of this phenomenon.

Niall: *Time is a construct of perception. You have heard it said that time flies when you are having fun or crawls when you have nothing to do. This* *is an oversimplification, however. With the proper application of focused perception, you can functionally change the way clock time works around you. I say "clock time" to delineate that which you experience when you use a timepiece to judge how many of your seconds or minutes have passed. Remember that what you believe manifests your reality. This is the basis for workings that involve clock time versus perceived time.*

Let us say that you wish to arrive at a destination within a certain range of clock minutes. If your perception is that time is limited and you have left yourself very few clock minutes in which to arrive somewhere, then the challenge of what you might call "bending" or "stretching" time becomes more difficult. Even so, you can experience time as stretching when you place yourself in a different mindset. Rather than traveling with the fear that you will not arrive on time, travel instead with a mental attitude of stillness. Allow yourself to feel that stillness deeply within, so that extraneous activity such as the ticking of a clock or the changing of electronic numbers on a display becomes meaningless to you. All moments become one moment. Thus, the moment in which you left your original location is the same as the moment in which you passed your halfway point, which is the same moment as the one in which you made a course correction, stopped for a traffic light, pulled into the parking lot you were trying to reach, and turned off your vehicle.

When you begin to experience this inner stillness and state of being suspended in one long moment, time begins to bend around you, and you may find that it takes you fewer clock minutes to arrive at your destination. It is not easy for people whose everyday reality is based on the clock or the calendar to learn to step aside from these artificial constructs and experience time as limitless instead of limited. But as with all things that relate directly to perception, energy, and the combination thereof, this may be learned with practice and persistence.

If you are going to practice this type of perception and eventually grasp the concept of allowing time to flow around you without affecting you, it is important to remember that no matter what may be going on in your immediate environment, a state of deep inner stillness is necessary to achieve the effect. If you become anxious or stressed about reaching your destination on time, your worry about being late is likely to become a self-fulfilling prediction. Time cannot flow around you unless you make of yourself an island of stillness, and this stillness can only come from within. It is not thought and rationalization to which time responds in this manner; thus, you cannot mentally enforce your will upon the clock. When time begins to stretch around you, it responds to what you feel, not to what you think.

Journal Entry, May 21, 2009

I bent time today. There is no other explanation for it. I left my house at 7:18 pm, very late for my writers' meeting, which had started at 6:30 pm. On the way there, I began musing about how the moment I was in was no different from the one I'd just been through, and no different from the one down the road in front of me. It was very peaceful. As I contemplated this, I drove as normal. Even if I'd been speeding, I would not have been able to drive the distance between my house and the meeting place in less than 20 minutes. Fifteen, at the very least, and that would be pushing it even without excess traffic. But when I arrived, I looked at my clock, and it read 7:26 pm, which means that I drove from my house to the meeting in eight minutes flat.

When told about this, my friend thought something must have been wrong with my car clock, but I checked it later against my cell phone clock, and they were running at the same time. No clock problem.

It's interesting when the song you're listening to on the radio or CD player plays itself at what appears to be normal speed, keeping track of the seconds and minutes as the time ticks by, but the clock on your car and cell phone don't seem to be running at the same time. For example, a three minute, twenty-four second song went by faster than the car and cell phone clocks, which only turned over maybe two minutes during the over-three-minute song.

This is not the first instance in which time has bent around me. The other day, I had several errands to run, and only about a half hour in which to make three stops, plus driving time, with several miles between each of the pertinent businesses. I headed off at 5:25 pm, needing to get to all three places before closing time at 6:00. I went through the credit union, deposited my check, drove on to the farmers' market, bought asparagus and exchanged pleasantries with the owner, then drove through busy traffic to the library.

During the whole trip, I was in what I call a "Mona Lisa" state of mind. Instead of being stressed, I was amused by everything that happened, even the three times I had to stomp on the brakes due to people slowing or stopping suddenly in front of me. None of the traffic issues that would normally have irritated me bothered me. I didn't even worry at all about what time it was. I pulled into the library parking lot at 5:58, just in time to grab the DVD they had on hold for me, right before they closed. I can bend time—at least once in a while. Wonder what will happen next?

Glamour and Perception

What exactly is glamour? In terms of magic, it is usually thought of as a complex illusion that alters the appearance of a person or object, often making it look—and sometimes feel—very different from the way it normally would. The lore surrounding faery glamour is couched in mystery, and seems to indicate that at least some tricks are being played with people's perception of what they see. Thus, according to lore, what a person perceives as a handful of gold from the world of Faerie often later proves to be nothing but a handful of stones or twigs, or a fancy gown is in fact an outfit made of rags.

While few humans are likely to be able to impose a vastly different mental image upon the mind of another person in a literal sense, I suspected that there were ways in which we could work our own type of personal "glamour" and be perceived in the way we wished to be. Niall explained to me that the way another person perceives us is largely due to the energy we project, and that a fundamental change in this projection can often bring about a vital change in the way we appear to others.

Niall: *Most people's perception is clouded. Few people see a thing as it truly is. Always, always, it is disguised by the veil of one's paradigms and beliefs. How, then, would you influence someone to perceive you as you wish them to? The concept of glamour is linked to that of perception. It is not possible to force another being to see you in a way that is completely alien to their paradigms. They will have no basis for comparison and no means by which to make sense of what they are seeing, except through the lens of their own* *beliefs and experiences. Even a sight that would seem at first totally outside one's experience is still filtered in this way. The brain immediately scrambles to put the unfamiliar sight into some sort of context. Glamour is an attempt to guide another into a perception that at least runs parallel to the image you were trying to project.*

Bear in mind that it is very hard to fool energy. If you are dealing with a person who is sensitive and relatively clear in his energy, he will tend to view you with a much cleaner lens. He will sense the energy you are putting out and he will perceive you accordingly. This is not a perception based on physicality, but on energetic resonance.

Thus, no matter how hard one may try to put across an image of competence and power, if the person being perceived does not feel himself to be competent and powerful, energy-sensitive people will tend to sense this and react with doubt. The dichotomy between the person's energy and his intended image will be apparent on an energetic level, and even if others cannot tell exactly what is wrong, they will still sense it. So the key to glamour, then, is to be able to harmonize your inner energies and your inner Knowing with the outward appearance you present and the overall impression you are trying to put across to others.

For example, if your energy is muted to the point where you are sending out the message that you are small and not to be noticed, in fact, many will tend to overlook you. Your perception of yourself as invisible similarly affects the perception of those around you, and if your projection of this energy is strong enough, you will find yourself overlooked and unnoticed.

This is not to say that if you were to dress in lurid colors or walk naked down the street while imagining yourself invisible, that you would remain unnoticed. If you were to do such a thing, you would most certainly not be projecting the energy of invisibility—rather the opposite, in fact. The invisible person is one who can blend seamlessly into any crowd, his energy kept close and muted, so that even if a person sees him they will not necessarily notice or remember that they did. Conversely, if you are dealing with a person whose energy so fills the space around him that he stifles and crowds others out, he will most certainly be noticed, and usually not in a favorable way.

Now, what about the energy of attraction? You have been around those whose energy is like a shining beacon, inspiring anyone within reach. These are often the performers from whom you cannot look away, or the public speakers who effortlessly hold the attention of their listeners. But there are other ways to use this attractive energy. Perhaps instead, this energy takes a gentler form, soothing and beckoning to those who are under stress or who feel pain. They find themselves attracted to the gentle energy of the healer, soothed by this person's very presence. This person may not even be particularly attractive on a physical level, but people will find themselves drawn nonetheless.

Do you see what we are speaking of here? Glamour does not necessarily have to be a kind of magic that causes visual illusion. Say, rather, that it is a kind of energy, and a way of projecting it. The way in which you use or hold your energy helps determine how people will respond to you. You perhaps dress for the role in which you wish to be seen, you project that energy, and people will tend to see, for the most part, what you intend them to see.

There are, of course, people who will never see you as you wish them to, no matter what energy you project and no matter how you dress or what credentials you present, but this is not due to a failing on your part. This is due to the fact that many people are simply not capable of seeing another's true appearance or sensing another's authentic energy, because the beholder's energy and perception is far too clouded. This kind of person tends to see others only through the very dusty lens of his own limited and faulty perception.

This is an unfortunate state of affairs, not only because it interferes with his ability to see others clearly, but also because it interferes with his ability to see himself clearly. No amount of glamour or projective energy will change the sight of this type of person, because he simply does not see others as they are, he sees them as he is. Until he changes himself and his energy from the inside, he will continue to see through a fogged window.

I have seen these principles involving energy and perception in action in my own life. In the past, whenever I perceived myself as a victim, others tended to treat me as such, despite what I believed were my efforts to discourage this behavior. I have also had the opposite experience.

Many years ago, I attended one of my first writers' conferences. I had a fairly good idea of how a professional businessperson was supposed to look, and I made an effort to present myself that way, following the "dress for success" motif. My clothing wasn't overstated; I wore a simple gray suit that wouldn't have stood out in any business crowd I could imagine. But what I also did in preparation for my day at the conference was put myself into a positive, confident mental attitude.

I told myself that I had gone there to make contacts, and I wished to be seen as a professional who could be respected, as well as someone with whom editors and agents would want to work. I tried to project a friendly and competent manner, and went into my activities with this attitude foremost. Although at that time I was far less familiar with the concepts of energy, auras, and the projection of such, I did get the feeling that I was putting out a certain image for others to see. I thought of it as "putting on my professional author hat."

Interesting things began to happen. Every agent or editor I spoke to agreed to look at my work, even when they had declined others only moments before. Image consultants approached me at random, convinced they could successfully promote my work and me, even when they found out that what I wrote wasn't the type of thing they normally promoted. My friend who had accompanied me to the conference seemed amazed at the regularity with which people stopped to speak with me, even when it seemed as though it must be obvious that I was not anyone important or anyone who could possibly help them advance their careers.

The oddest occurrence was when I had the chance to speak with a well-known author I'd admired for years. Most pros are happy to speak to new writers at conferences, so the fact that he gave me a few minutes of his time was not unusual. What was unusual was what happened afterward. After I'd spoken with the author, I became aware that someone was standing behind me. I presumed that she was waiting to speak with the author as well, so I excused myself in order to give her a chance to do so.

Imagine my surprise when she explained that she wasn't waiting to speak with him; she was waiting to speak with me! She didn't even know why, she said. She told me that she just had the feeling I was someone with whom she should make contact. Bemused, I gave her my business card and took hers, and we each went on our way. Interestingly enough, I never heard from her again. It seemed she was drawn into my sphere on that day only.

The Power of Names

Anyone who has read faery lore has no doubt heard references to the power of names. Folklore, mythology and popular modern fiction all tend to repeat the same concept—that so-called "true names" are powerful and can sometimes be used to summon or affect their owners in some way. Unfortunately, there doesn't seem to be much information about just how and why this is so. Naturally, I asked Niall for information on the subject.

Niall: *To name something is to define it, and so to attempt to set limits upon it. But what most often happens is that by naming it, you only manage to limit your own perception of it. Unless the thing or being you tried to name takes these definitions to heart and makes them part of itself, it will remain unlimited and the only limits will be on you and on your ability to understand it fully. Why would you want to limit your perception of something or someone? Limited perception, labels, and incorrect definitions lead to misunderstandings and disharmony. These things in turn lead to conflict.*

Humans like to name things, to develop a fixed perception of something and encourage others to perceive it the same way. You prefer that all matter and other entities be classified, sorted, and filed. You organize your perceptions in the same way you organize so many other facets of your lives, into neat rows and boxes. You think that doing this will help you to know a thing or being's place in the universe, or at least its place in relationship to yourselves, and in this way, you think to understand its nature. But without realizing it, you are limiting yourselves by exercising this need to put names to or categorize everything and everyone.

An inadequate name or definition may be, in part, a truth. But names as definitions tend to be too narrow to encompass that to which they are given, and much knowing is lost in the translation.

Even personal names seek to define people in a particular way, but your system of naming is flawed. A personal or use name is not as effective as it once was, and has lost most of its power and significance. For example, at one time, the name "Cooper" meant a barrel maker, and there might be only one to any given village. Now, many people bear the surname Cooper, and yet very few if any of them actually make barrels. Nor does the name Cooper tell you anything about one's personality, his sense of humor, or her tenderness or compassion.... I could go on, but you get the idea. The name tells you nothing. All it serves to do is to allow you to classify that person as a being separate from others, and even that often fails. How many bear the name "John Smith" in the world today? How will you know one John Smith from another? Not by the name; that is certain.

You recognize an individual by the unique set of characteristics he or she exhibits, by his or her unique vibration, manner of speaking, or physical appearance in this lifetime. Names are interchangeable, but the beings who bear those names are unique. "Use" names are only that—for common use—and easily enough discarded when you cease to play the role assigned to that name and appearance.

Also, bear in mind that most of you did not name yourselves; someone else named you. The name you were given at birth may or may not suit the unique essence that you are. Personal or use names are of scant significance when you think in terms of multiple lifetimes. You have been known by many different use names over the centuries, and none of them are correct. None of them are the true resonance of your spirit. This is where the difference between a use name and a true name comes into play.

Though we are all connected at the Spirit level, each individual emanation of Spirit has a unique resonance or energy signature that defines it. This is really what is being referred to when someone speaks of a true name. If you knew the original pure note of resonance or "true name" of a being, you might in fact manage to introduce some disharmony into that resonance, which could then alter it if you had the means by which to coerce the being into changing its perception of itself.

Many beings have been corrupted or changed from their original natures. Humans are often apt examples of this. Many have allowed the resonances with which they first emanated into being, which we will here refer to as their true names, to be altered or lost over time. A person either forgets his original state of being, or is talked into believing his true nature to be different—in essence, he changes himself or allows himself to be changed to fit a narrower or vastly altered definition, and this alters his energy. He may spend many lifetimes trying to figure out who or what he is supposed to be, and he is constantly surrounded by others who try to further define him according to their own limited perceptions.

(Here, the information took on a more personal note.)

If I told you your true name, would you recognize it? I know that in your present state, you do not remember it. You once thought that if you did not remember your true name, then you must be safe, for you would not inadvertently reveal it to anyone who might use its power against you. Unfortunately, you lost the memory a long time ago, so your reasoning is flawed. You have already allowed yourself to be altered. Every time you allow someone else's erroneous perception of you to change your view of yourself, you are altered further. But lately, you have begun to undo much of this damage. If you continue on this path, you will eventually see your original patterns emerge, until you find your spirit in increasingly familiar territory. You will eventually recover your memory of exactly who and what you are, and your true resonance will return to you. Once you own its power, you can make of yourself anything you wish. The one being who can use your true name either for or against you, is you.

And before you officially ask—no, I cannot tell you your true name. Let us assume for one moment that I actually know it. Even if I do, my revealing it to you would constitute a breach of contract. You allowed yourself to forget it. You allowed yourself to be altered. Part of your purpose is to reconnect, to heal, to reintegrate. I cannot and will not circumvent that process or cheapen your efforts by helping you to cheat on this lesson. I can help you in many ways, but this is not one of them. I would not be helping you if I did reveal it, because the very act of doing so would alter you and alter the destiny you chose for yourself.

Ask me instead to spend time with you, take away your headache or put you to sleep; those things I can do. Besides, how many women usually complain that their loved ones don't pay enough attention to the little things?

Me: Very funny. But I understand, and you're right. I take great comfort from you being just the way you are. You are the most stable thing in my world, my lodestone, my true north. I didn't know just how much I craved stability until you spoke up and began to teach me all this. I know that sounds odd, seeing that I'm speaking of a being whose form is fluid and changeable.

Niall: *My outer form may be changeable, beloved, but my essential nature is not. It is that which you correctly perceive as stable, for in essence, the Sidhe have changed very little since we came into being. It is no wonder that in a human form, you would find this stability comforting. But what you must remember is that your own perception of your life as chaotic creates the chaos you experience.*

Perceive your essence as stable, and you will find that you can be your own anchor. You are your own true north, your own lodestone. Do not give your personal power away, even to me. Think of me as an equal, and celebrate our ability to be together. Take comfort in us, but take equal comfort in yourself. You are not lacking in any of these abilities. You are not less. Anything I can do, you can do. All you need do is relearn, remember, and reconnect.

CHAPTER SIX

HUMAN AND SIDHE RELATIONSHIPS

Sitting in on various classes and discussions, I have found that there is a great deal of curiosity about the experience of human/Sidhe relationships, especially romantic ones. The great variance in folkloric and historic personal accounts of these relationships led me to ask Niall to help clarify some of the seeming discontinuity.

To begin, I had to ask about the notion of humans and spirit beings engaging in intimate relationships with each other in the first place. This has often been a taboo subject, and has been the object of much debate, as opinions about sexual intimacy with spirits tend to fall into one of two camps—those who believe it enhances a person's spiritual growth and those who believe that it is either erroneous or impossible.

Let's Talk About Sex

Me: Why is it that so much of today's esoteric literature tends to state that if one is to advance spiritually, one should suppress the desire for sex and not ascribe any romantic ideas to a relationship with a guide or anyone else on a different plane? Why is the idea of two entities on separate planes of existence carrying on a romance so presumably "less advanced" or "lower energy" than if there was no romantic component?

Niall: *This is a very complex question. One reason is that connecting so deeply to another being, as during the sexual act, requires a certain loss of control. It requires subsuming oneself to the merging, the blending, the union. Thus two become, in effect, one. It is this very loss of control that many people fear will lead to non-spiritual impulses or a lowering of vibration. What so many do not realize is that in order to fully merge with another, it requires a raising of vibration to a point which, if done right, both resonate as one. In effect, two merged beings speak with one note, one voice. There is no higher vibration than that of oneness at this level.*

Desire is not, in itself, at all detrimental to this sort of merging. It is simply that, when the moment of bliss which you know as orgasm occurs, some people pull away or hoard the energy released so that instead of a moment of oneness, it becomes a moment of separation. It might be said that those who view the intimate act of merging as a lower-vibration act simply do not know how to do it right. As with anything of value, it takes practice and must be approached with reverence.

Rather than work hard to reach a level at which complete union is possible, some would rather avoid the act altogether. They assume that because of the separation and pulling away that sometimes occurs if one becomes distracted by the orgasm itself, sex must then be a lower function. This pulling away occurs when people strive for the orgasm instead of relaxing into the merging, and then the orgasm becomes an end in itself, instead of the merging being the main point of the interaction. When the merging is done right, however, orgasm occurs naturally as a result. Do you see the distinction? It is a difference in intent and focus, in motivation.

Me: Why would some rather avoid sex at that level?

Niall: *There are any number of reasons. Because of its difficulty, because of the time and effort involved, because at that stage of intimacy, it is simply not possible for one partner to hide anything from the other. Or, in some cases, because of a misfired view of sex as non-spiritual, mostly due to conventions imposed on human beliefs by religion.*

There is also the view some have of things relating to the body, to the earthy or physical nature as being non-spiritual. It is not that physical things are non-spiritual. It is simply that they can be a distraction, because many people do not see beyond the surface nature of a thing. When you begin to view all things as multidimensional, physical and spiritual manifestations of being both at the same time, you will see not only the polarity inherent in it, but also the wholeness and integration.

Guilt over physical things comes, in part, from the very separation and fragmentation that so many suffer from today. Once you begin to function as a multidimensional being, you have no need for the guilt, and no need for the idea that physicality is something you must "rise above."

Me: What about the angels, or beings from the angelic realm, who are often said to indicate that they don't need sex at all?

Niall: *Some beings truly do not need merging of this sort, and because they are of such a different order of being, they do not perceive that as having value. If one were accustomed to embracing all of creation at once, one might not see the need to embrace just one other at a time, on a level of intimacy that is so private, so exclusive. Such beings might see this as a waste of time and energy. Others may not.*

Me: How do the Sidhe tend to see it?

Niall: *When the act of sex becomes a greater means of connection, a means by which two beings who have reached a particular level of intimacy with one another might more fully connect to each other's* *essence, then sex becomes something else. It becomes not a means to some vague titillation and fleeting sensatory experience of bliss, but instead becomes a sacrament, an experience of union on a microcosmic level.*

In this, the union of two is a smaller enactment of the far greater act of becoming one with All That Is. It is an expression of love in the fullest measure and in one of its most sacred forms, for it embodies all the energy of the moment of creation. Surely, there can be no higher work than this. It is not the act that makes the difference, beloved, but the intention. There is no higher purpose than the fullest expression of love, and when that takes the form of two becoming one, the energy expressed in such an act is transcendent.

There is nothing wrong with having sex. There is nothing wrong with abstaining. There is, however, something wrong with withholding love or the expression thereof. The main thing one must be aware of is whether it is indeed love that is being expressed, or simply a need for stimulation or a cure for the loneliness that comes with disconnection. If you are fully connected to another and wish to express that connection through a more intimate act such as lovemaking, then there is nothing wrong with that choice, even if your lover currently inhabits a different plane of being than you do. Love and the expression of love takes so many forms that to restrict and limit it is a detriment.

In other words, if you do not have sex simply because you do not choose to do so, but love is still fully and richly expressed, then that is fine. But if you are in a relationship which would otherwise be sexually intimate and you do not engage in sex (which in this case would rightfully be termed "making love") because of feelings of guilt or of adherence to rules set by another, then such abstinence would be a detriment to both entities involved.

Relationships

Over the years, I've heard stories referring to relationships between humans and faeries. Some of these accounts were related in Celtic legend, and some dated from the medieval period and later. Very few of them seemed to end particularly well. Even today, widespread belief seems to be that faery and human relationships are possible, but that they operate under restrictions that, if violated, are said to end the relationship immediately.

I am not sure exactly how these beliefs developed; many of them seem to have been passed down via oral stories that were only committed to writing much later, far after the fact. We all know how the game of "telephone" ends; by the time the message makes its whispered way from the originator to the last person in the line of recipients, it has usually been so altered from the original version as to be unrecognizable. Seeking some current perspective, I asked Niall for his take on the subject.

Me: Can you tell me why romantic relationships between "faeries" and humans have often been perceived as so fraught with danger or difficulty? Do they truly most often end in disaster?

(At this point, a surge of wordless idea/concepts flashed into my mind at lightning speed, followed by a pause in which Niall seemed to back up and start over.)

Niall: *There is so much here you need to understand that I am having difficulty not conveying it to you all at once, in one jumbled mass.*

To begin with, humans and Sidhe often have a different understanding of love. In human relationships, people bind themselves with a set of rules, prohibitions and limits—there is that word again!—which force love to take a preconceived form. You are taking the most unlimited force in the universe and trying to make it follow a set of laws. By human terms, if these rules or laws are ever bent or broken, it often instigates a breakup and the denial of love, not to mention years or even lifetimes of pain.

It is very difficult for the Sidhe to take such an unlimited thing as love and force it to conform to the rules and limits humans set on it. The lore many refer to involving human/Sidhe relationships most often cites instances in which a human woman or man was taken into our realm or encountered by one of us in your realm, made love to, and subsequently deserted. Other stories cite instances in which the Sidhe lover insisted on certain taboos which were not to be broken, and then the human inadvertently broke them and was, again, deserted. This is the basis of the common belief that the Sidhe are cold, fickle and unforgiving of mistakes. Yet our experience is that love is in fact limitless. In order to explain this seeming paradox, we must look deeper at relationships and what they are meant to accomplish.

A relationship, whether romantic or platonic, is meant to be supportive and joyous to both partners on many levels. Yet what too often happens in human relationships is that one partner begins to form unrealistic expectations of the other, and perceives any failure to meet those expectations as a betrayal. Disagreements are blown out of proportion and grievances are nursed to the extent that they begin to fester within the spirits who house them.

Many people begin a relationship with the expectation that their needs will be met, that the prospective lover will fill a gap or hole within one's being. Any possible hint of what is perceived as unfaithfulness or neglect is met with extreme hurt, anger and hostility on the part of the one who believes himself wronged. Trust is eroded and the relationship dies a premature death before the deeper levels of love are ever reached. As with nearly everything we have discussed, perception is the key. Fear of loss and fear of betrayal often lead to those very happenings, driving lovers apart.

They begin to see each other as hateful or fatally flawed, and all the energy surrounding their relationship begins to vibrate with fear.

Given that this type of perception happens so easily among humans, any Sidhe who enters into a romantic relationship with one takes a great risk. There is the risk that overtures will be misinterpreted, that human lovers will wish to place the same restrictions on us that they place on themselves, and that at the first test of love or the first disagreement, the human will react in fear and assume that he or she is no longer loved or wanted. If either partner makes assumptions based on fear and insecurity, the vibrations of fear will enter into what is supposed to be a harmonic resonance greater than any other. And yet, many of us would gladly risk any of these possibilities if we felt that the human in question would be able to enter the relationship with an open mind and an open heart.

An important thing to remember is that loss is illusion. Unfortunately, it is an illusion that humans give in to all too readily, and many Sidhe do not know how to respond to it. True resonance between beings cannot be achieved if one of those beings is fearful or limited in his perceptions.

Love should be given wholeheartedly and with one's entire being, and should never be given with unrealistic expectations. It is also true that the type of resonance to which we referred cannot be achieved if one partner seeks to alter the other to suit his or her own perception of how the other should be.

It is true that there have been instances in which a Sidhe lover set certain conditions by which the human lover was asked to abide. Usually these conditions were meant to prevent the human from placing certain judgments or behavioral standards on their Sidhe partner. The requests were not made for the purpose of changing the human, but for determining whether he or she would be able to understand our way of being and comprehend why it is important to live and love without judgment. If two beings are not well matched, no amount of rule-making will compensate, and if this is the case, then it is best that each be set free to love elsewhere.

Me: Is it true that the Sidhe do not always practice monogamy? Many humans have a perception of faeries as being unlike humans in their morals and relationship ethics.

Niall: *Yes, and this is a good thing! A word on the concepts of promiscuity and unfaithfulness: Humans have what we would consider a double standard. Before entering into the formal contract that you know as marriage, many humans share emotional connections with multiple partners. But once a pair begins to develop the relationship to a deeper, more meaningful level, they begin to place restrictions on the sharing of love with anyone other than the primary partner. This, you term monogamy.*

Many humans are so jealous that they stifle their lover and will not tolerate the lover even looking at another person with anything approaching sexual interest, much less genuine affection. In part, this is due to fear of loss of the primary partner's love, but it is also because when you reincarnate into a new physical form, you forget that you have loved many others over the course of many lifetimes.

Did you stop loving the others simply because you and they are incarnated into different bodies, different illusions? No. Love is not meant to be limited to single human lifetimes only. If you were suddenly confronted physically with all the spouses you contracted with from your past six or seven lifetimes and could actually remember those lifetimes, you would have no idea what to do with all the emotion and feelings of connection you have to these people. You would be thrown into a state of confusion.

This seems to be a limitation of 3-D consciousness, which sees resources as finite. But since the Sidhe are aware that love is in fact unlimited, we do not perceive a situation in which we would be unable to fully love or support any romantic partner we have ever become involved with. Because such support is readily available, jealousy is not something we usually experience either.

This is not to say that we tend to seek out multiple partners just for the thrill of it, or for relief from boredom or dissatisfaction. Many of us are happily committed to a single partner. However, in cases where true romantic love is felt for more than one, we have no need to experience the fear, lack of support, or sense of betrayal that humans experience under similar circumstances.

For one thing, if you know that it is possible truly to love more than one romantic partner at the same time, then the emotion of jealousy becomes unnecessary and all parties are fully supported. Also, many of us have the ability literally to be in more than one place at the same time. Consciousness itself is unlimited, so you could easily direct your consciousness to several places or to several people at once, and still be yourself, still remain fully aware in every instance.

Even now, your scientists are beginning to understand the concepts of multiple levels of being, of multiple universes and the possibility of living in multiple realities all at the same time. You are only as limited as you believe yourself to be, so if you choose to believe that love is finite, then you will tend to experience fear of loss when it relates to love.

Do you see why carrying on a long-term romantic relationship with a human can be problematic? If the human is able to see past the illusion of limitation, then such unions can be amazingly supportive and successful for both partners. But if the human begins to place limitations on either the expression of love or on the actions and the very being of the Sidhe lover, then what often happens is that the Sidhe will eventually be forced to concede and withdraw. We are not accustomed to living with the sort of limitations you habitually impose on yourselves, and it can be heartbreaking for us to watch you do it. Sometimes the only solution is to leave you to your illusions of loss; but be assured that we experience deep regret whenever it happens.

Me: Could you speak a little about the notion that Sidhe lovers don't like to stick around with humans when their bodies begin to age?

Niall: (smiles at this) *How many times must I repeat the word perception? Aging is something that humans have chosen for themselves, and perhaps one day they will see it as unnecessary and remember how to cease to do it. I suppose if there were any Sidhe who desired only to have physical sexual contact with humans and never take the relationship further, they might not have reason to stay around once the human had begun to succumb to the illusion of age. But the reality is that we do not tend to want humans only for sex! We are accustomed to engaging in intimacy that is far more than just physical. There are so many more levels of interaction possible that limiting oneself to just the physical is, frankly, boring.*

So, when we engage fully into an intimate relationship with a human, we want to interact on the energetic and spiritual levels, involving a mingling of essences and a merging of spirit that far exceeds any type of physical sex most humans are used to. Tantra is probably the closest concept you have to the type of energetic exchange to which I refer, in a sexual sense. But sexual union is only one of many ways in which resonance and harmony of spirit can be expressed by two beings who desire to experience love with each other.

A true union occurs on several energetic levels at once, and once entered into, is never taken lightly. Such relationships are of very long duration; one might even call them eternal, unless something happens to change the essential harmonic of the relationship. Among the Sidhe, this type of change does not tend to happen often, but when you throw a human into the mix, the dynamic can be a bit different, due to the human's potential for more rapid change.

HUMAN AND SIDHE RELATIONSHIPS

So, when we look at humans, we are looking at far more than just your physical bodies. We see you on more than one energetic level. A being's unique energy and vibration is what we truly attune to, and this does not have to change with the aging of a 3-D body.

To bring a lengthy explanation to a close, no, it does not matter to most of us whether you age physically or not, so long as your energy remains unimpaired. In fact, that energy becomes ever clearer and more beautiful as you move further into wholeness over the course of several lifetimes. It is like watching the most miraculous unfolding of an exotic flower, and we never tire of marveling at it when it happens.

It is worth pointing out that we are not usually attracted to humans whose energy is extremely dense and muddied. If your spirits are in the process of integration and therefore your energy and vibration is rising, we would be much more likely to take notice. From there, it is much like the progression of any relationship, but with far fewer limits. Humans who are most closely attuned to our nature and resonance would likely find it easier to meet us on these levels than those whose energies are primarily focused on the purely physical dimensions and experiences. Those who have said that the higher a vibration you have, the higher level an entity you can attract to you are correct.

Me: I have heard lore of Sidhe bringing humans physically into your realm with you. Could you tell me whether this happens often, and if it does, then how does that affect the relationship, etc?

Niall: *This used to happen earlier on in the course of human history. However, it rarely happens now because of the growth of technology, and the logic that tells you we don't exist.* (smiles) *If one of us were to bring a human lover into our dimension physically, that would not be particularly helpful to the relationship unless the human were quite well attuned to us and to the nature of our existence.*

Let us suppose that a Sidhe were to bring a human lover—physicality and all—into our world. Humans often cannot acclimate well to the dimensional shift because their original vibrations were not high enough for them to get here on their own while still in their physical bodies. Because of this, much of their energy remains attuned to their former 3-D reality. Can you see where this is heading? In cases such as this, the only way to prevent much discomfort on the humans' part and allow them to continue to develop spiritually at their own pace would be to return them to their own world. And of course, the return to the third dimension would then cause them to doubt their experiences in our world and wonder what it was that truly happened.

Now, it has been the case on occasion that a human was able to acclimate to our reality and chose willingly to stay here with us. In these instances, special dispensation was made for this, if it seemed that the change would cause no problem for the human. However, in most cases, if a human is brought into the higher planes by another and does not have the chance to evolve and move to a higher vibratory level on his or her own, there is a certain element missing from that human's energy and resonance. All these things must be taken into consideration whenever such a monumental decision is made.

Me: Do you have any advice for those humans who desire to form intimate romantic relationships with Sidhe?

Niall: *Work to become the kind of person you desire to attract to you. If you wish a higher-level relationship, raise your vibration. If you would have someone who is kind and understanding, be kind and understanding. Humans are capable of the same high-level interactions among themselves as those that the Sidhe experience with one another.*

It is important that humans do not think all their problems will be solved if they are able to enter into a love relationship with one of the Sidhe or

HUMAN AND SIDHE RELATIONSHIPS

with a member of any other higher-dimensional race. Any interaction is only as strong as the weaker partner, and one partner should not become an enabler or a means of compensation for the other. If a human does in fact form a romantic relationship with a Sidhe or vice versa, both partners can expect to engage in a great deal of hard work—perhaps even harder work than if they had fallen in love with another person originally closer to their own vibration.

For a human, entering into a love match with a Sidhe involves change on so many levels that it often figuratively turns his or her life upside down. A person desiring such a relationship should never seek one out of the need for validation, the desire for an ego boost, or out of a materialistic need for gain or gratification. Indeed, no one of any race or kind should ever seek to enter any relationship with those motivations, which can lead to delusions of the worst sort. Love is the most sacred expression of connection between beings, and should always be treated as such.

Humans can have the strongest and truest of relationships possible if they simply engage fully with each other and let go of the judgments and crippling expectations that too often occur. A fully realized human/human relationship is not at all inferior to a human/Sidhe relationship, nor yet a Sidhe/Sidhe relationship. Fully realized love between any two beings is transcendent, no matter the origin of the participants.

What makes a relationship special is not the fame, color, dimension of origin or exotic nature of either partner, but the quality and beauty of the love expressed within the union. Our best advice here would be to love wholeheartedly and engage with others in full understanding and acceptance of their natures. Enter relationships without preconceived notions, and seek to be the kind of lover you desire to attract. If both partners—of any kind—do these things, then no matter how much work may need to go into it, no relationship will ever be unfulfilling. Instead, it will be an unfolding and celebration of pure joy and pure light.

CHAPTER SEVEN

LIFE AND THE AFTERLIFE

For decades, the question of what life might be like in another dimension has often been deemed worthy subject matter for science fiction or fantasy stories. But the reality of life in the Otherworld, as shown to me by Niall and my other Sidhe contacts, is far more vital and wondrous than I could have imagined. I was able to experience some of it myself via dreamwalks and meditations, and Niall's conversations have also given me a fascinating window into life beyond this plane of existence.

Multidimensional

Me: Before the Sidhe went into the Otherworld, you lived here, in this dimension. Were you physical beings then?

Niall: *Very much so. In a sense, we are still physical beings, just as in another sense, we are not. It depends upon your frame of reference. Early on in our development, many of us learned to alter our physicality so that we were capable of entering other realms of being as well. Not all of us* *could do this at first, but we had our wise ones and teachers who learned and then shared their knowledge with us.*

Me: From things you've said at times, it sounds like you do have access to the various senses when living in a nonphysical reality—taste, scent, touch, etc. Is that correct?

Niall: *It is not so much that we live in a nonphysical reality as that our physicality is constituted differently from yours. We can be as solid to each other on our plane of reality as you are to others who share your plane. This is why when you dreamwalked to me in the Otherworld, you perceived me as being solid to the touch.*

Now, with regard to the senses: yes, we are very much aware of such things as taste, touch, scent, sound and appearance. But the benefit of being in a dimension with a higher vibratory rate is that our experience of these basic senses is much more complete. We comprehend much larger visual and aural spectrums than you do, and all of our other senses are intensified as well.

When you take form in the third dimension, you cut yourself off from a complete experience of the senses, and only a fraction of the possible input actually translates through to you via your sensory organs. When your physical senses are dulled, you must learn to rely on nonphysical means in order to perceive and experience things more fully. We are aware that this is difficult when your society tells you not to believe in that which you cannot see and touch. But once you realize how limited your senses are, and are able to open yourself to experience things through more than just your physical reality, your understanding will increase greatly. In essence, your senses will be extended through the vehicle of your non-physical perception.

Me: Can you speak about the reasons why the Sidhe departed from this dimension?

Niall: *The relationship between humans and Sidhe has always been complicated. There were times when we thought we might be able to get along peaceably, but there were also times of conflict. Much depended on the prevailing human culture during the periods in question.*

Humans reproduce more readily than we do and their expansion across the globe continued to increase. When they began to come into the areas to which we had removed ourselves and vie for resources there, we saw that soon we would no longer be able to avoid the conflicts that arose as a result. As the Otherworld and many of its adjoining realms were familiar to us and indeed some of our ancestors had come from there previously, many of our groups began to return there to dwell. Some stayed in the earth realm as long as possible before leaving.

When in the midst of any conflict, it is always vital to consider what is best for the majority of the people involved, on either side. Since humans could not physically move into the Otherworld or its environs on their own but the Sidhe could, it was decided that our withdrawal was the best way to stave off further conflict.

This was done with a long-term view, as we knew it was possible that one day, our two peoples might be able to establish a rapport and useful communication between us. In order for that to happen, the Sidhe were better off to simply remove ourselves from the conflict and await the time when things would change.

Me: We've briefly touched on the notion of humans being taken to live among the Sidhe before, but it sounded as though that was a complicated thing. Can you explain a little more about how it is possible for one accustomed to this physical state of being to exist in a dimension such as yours?

Niall: *If a human were to come and live with us on a permanent basis, he would most likely come to us after his death, and would then choose not to go* *back into a new body in the third dimension. But in order for a human soul to truly become one of us, he would need to be well attuned to us and fully committed to the type of existence we experience.*

As we have mentioned elsewhere, many humans don't find that this works for them; they are on a different path of development, and find that if they short-circuit the process, they have left parts of themselves elsewhere, yet unrecovered and nonintegrated. This accounts for the feeling of discontent some humans have when they try to live in our world. In those cases, they retain the nagging sense that there is something they have not done, something they left behind in the human realm. And indeed they did leave something behind—the remaining fragmented parts of themselves and their energies.

Many of us foresee a day when humans and Sidhe will walk openly together. Others are still cautious, unsure whether humans will rise to the occasion of embracing other beings, other species not of a 3-D physical reality. Many humans still have difficulty getting along with each other. They are often afraid of the ghosts and spirits of their own kind. How would they deal with entire races of beings beyond their usual understanding of existence?

It is for those who can attune more closely to our energy and vibrations to help build the connections that will bridge our two modes of existence. When this happens, we will all experience change on a deep, vital level, and the harmony of all creation will begin to re-form and reintegrate.

Me: Do you think it possible that most humans will become multidimensional beings at some point?

Niall: *I think it entirely possible. In essence, they already are multidimensional beings; they just do not always remember. There is nothing the Sidhe have learned that humans cannot learn as well. Indeed, some individual humans have long since moved on to a conscious* *multidimensional state. Some have discarded their physicality and become guides to others, and some have moved on to entirely new experiences and modes of being.*

The key here is where people choose to focus their efforts, and whether they are willing to keep at the process for long enough to allow such an integral change to happen. I think we will see many more moving along this road in the future, as they become increasingly discontent with the standards and mores practiced by their present society.

That is one reason for incarnation into a strongly physical dimension; it brings things and ideas into such an overt state of manifestation that it forces people to closely evaluate their reasons for creating the realities they create, and to learn what works and what doesn't. It is a rich ground for experimentation and learning, and gives a vivid experience of cause and consequence.

Contradictions in Paradigms

Over the years, I've seen a great variety of interpretations of the appearance, nature, or typical interactions people have with Sidhe or any being that could be classified as "faery." I've read accounts that date from several centuries ago to more recently, and while there are some definite similarities among them, there are some definite differences, too.

When I first began to have my own experiences with the Sidhe, it worried me that my perceptions of them sometimes differed greatly from some of those I'd read about. I noted that standard warnings seemed to accompany many of the older folk beliefs about the faeries, advising cautions that I hadn't necessarily been taking or indicating dangers that I hadn't sensed. Of course, it is also true that any two people's experience of the same thing can be perceived very differently by each.

As my own experience with Niall had shown me a far different view of the Sidhe than many of the old tales indicated, this occasioned some discussion about perception itself, and the necessarily subjective nature of any interaction with the Sidhe or fae of any kind.

Me: Is the fact that humans tend to see things through the filter of their own paradigms part of why people have passed down frightening stories of the Sidhe and of faeries over the centuries?

Niall: *In part. There is truth to the idea that people tend to label as frightening those things for which they can find no clear reference or context; there is a prevalent human idea that what seems different must be something to be feared or viewed as a possible threat. This concept of otherness is what keeps many groups at odds with each other, and it is a situation that must be rectified if there is ever to be peace on a larger scale.*

There is also truth in the notion that not all experiences humans have had with the Sidhe historically have been entirely benign. The first frightening stories stemmed from our species' early encounters with each other, complicated by misunderstandings. Over the intervening centuries, there have been instances of unpleasant interactions between us. Some of this is due to human perception clouded by fear, and some of it is due to the early decision of the Sidhe to maintain ourselves out of harm's way.

In certain cases, humans' fear of us tended to keep them at a distance, and there were (and to some extent still are) those of us who felt a continued need for caution. In the instances in which we capitalized on the limitations of human perception, we usually did so out of self-preservation. As you have seen in your own dealings between human groups and governments, there can be a certain usefulness in being perceived as something to be feared. There have been times when we made use of that, just as humans often have and still do.

The problem with these early interactions is that people's stories of us were so pervasive that they lent themselves readily to use for explaining any frightening or otherwise unexplainable phenomenon. Many otherwise harmless incidents and even a few humorous pranks were rapidly blown out of all proportion, and soon we were being blamed for everything from sickly children to sour milk, even when these were none of our doing. (Shrug.) This is what happens when fear is allowed to cloud perception.

We have never said that we never made mistakes. Mistakes were made by both groups, human and Sidhe. We are not perfect, nor would we make such a claim. But even in mistakes, wisdom can be gained, so that such mistakes need never be repeated.

The challenge now is for everyone to rise above limited perceptions and paradigms and embrace a more harmonious state of being. If all beings are to expand their perceptions and be open to interactions with other species and races, then they will need to discard their notions of otherness, which are limiting beliefs that keep us divided.

Me: This question relates to perceptions and paradigms in a slightly different sense. Why would Christian mystics find a way to explain the Sidhe or at least the concept of faeries in their model, but the Sidhe don't seem to speak much of angels, just "higher beings?"

It seems the more mystically-minded Christians have ways to explain faeries and integrate them into their belief systems, but the Sidhe don't seem to worry about integrating the angelic/Judeo Christian belief system into who and what they are, despite the folk tales about faeries being not-quite-fallen angels. So how and where do the two paradigms intersect—or do they? And is such an intersection even necessary?

Niall: *It stands to reason that Sidhe and humans might perceive the same thing differently. One person's higher being is another person's angel. Each receives information in a form easiest for him to handle.*

If a person starts out from any particular paradigm at all, he will often fear to release it entirely when confronted with new or contradictory information. Fitting the Sidhe or the fae into one's Christian or other religious worldview is better than disbelieving in us altogether. We would far rather be perceived as some kind of angels than the rather disturbing alternative, though we are neither.

You have arrived at the place where you are willing to set aside all your previous models for belief and make the leap, like your blind cat who leaps off the ottoman or bed without being able to see the floor beneath him. He simply knows the floor will be there, and that he will land safely. The possibility of not doing so does not occur to him. This is the essence of Knowing.

Faith, the precursor to Knowing, is not necessarily the absence of doubt. Rather, faith is the ability to proceed without having all the pieces of the puzzle, or to continue on the journey with part of the map still missing. You believe in our existence, and you have taken it a step further, declaring your love for us without reservation. This has not gone unnoticed. We can feel what you feel, and through you, we know what it is to walk partially blinded. Your willingness to provide us with this window is of great value to us, and we will not forget. Others have done the same, and in the days to come, more will follow. By this means, we may begin to bridge the gap of communication between human and Sidhe.

Do not concern yourself with the differences between your experience of us and the ways in which others who believe in what they call nature spirits choose to frame their ideas. It is a subjective experience, which you must expect in a world where form can be fluid.

Rigidity in belief is of no use to us, for what is brittle will break. Trust that your experience of us is real, and that others' experiences are real also even if they seem different, for much as your brain translates our language into that which you can understand, so too does people's esoteric experience translate into a form or paradigm which they can accept. As humans learn and grow, so too will their perception, until one day they may see us as we truly are. I think such a day will not come until they have learned to see themselves as they truly are as well, but that is a matter for each individual to address when he is prepared to do so.

The concepts of superiority and inferiority must be set aside. The idea of credentials is a construct of the human ego, and counts for little in the other dimensions of existence. You have read of dimensions where the ego disappears altogether. Indeed, these are the realms of higher beings, but not places for which most people are ready. For now, know that the notion of ego and credentials is illusion, much as form is illusion.

You are a storyteller, so you will understand when we say that these credentials, positions, and appointments are stories that beings tell themselves in an attempt to explain their origins and their very existence. They provide a frame of reference in which a person places himself. When one reaches a level of harmonious interaction with all other beings, the need for these stories becomes obsolete/unnecessary.

Reincarnation

Not everyone believes in the concept of having more than one lifetime, but it is not a new belief. Some cultures have accepted it as a matter of course for millennia. Nowadays, more and more evidence in favor of reincarnation comes to light from many different sources.

Past life regressions are one such indicator, but also compelling are spontaneous memories that surface in young children and cannot otherwise be explained. Oftentimes, such memories are vividly detailed—so much so that they are verifiable through research into the specifics that the children recall, such as dates, names of past-life family members, and more.

One day, curious about how the Sidhe might view reincarnation, I asked Niall whether he had any insight on that subject for human beings. He responded with:

While you are in a physical body, you often do not conceive of yourselves as being real in any other form. The physical is all you perceive, though there are many levels of being beyond that of the third dimension. The very act of taking a physical form with a new brain, new cells and genetics, takes away your surface memory of ever being other. This is one reason many of you fear death, as you are not certain what becomes of the being you know as yourself after it transitions out of a physical body.

Each transition into physical form is but a continuation of the same journey—what you would consider the journey of your spirit. For you, this repeated transitioning into and out of physical form can be both a blessing and a curse, because it allows you the illusion that you are something new, that the slate is wiped clean with each lifetime and you can start over.

This is a challenge we Sidhe do not often have to face, as we stay indefinitely in the one state and rarely cross over into the other. Were we to periodically confine ourselves in new physical bodies as humans do, we would experience the same things—the temporary forgetting of who and what we are, and the sense that we have started over. This is not usually our way.

As we progressed in our development, we learned to bear the burden of all our actions throughout centuries and millennia. It helps when past, present and future are not perceived as separate times, but all encompassed in the one existence. What we are now, we were then, and will be.

For yourselves, the consequence of ending the cycles of repeated forgetfulness would be to remember every mistake, every act of violence, and every deed that you might find cause to regret. But it would also be to remember every kindness, every act of faith or love, every perfect moment of beauty.

If you eventually choose to forego the process of repetition, of forgetting, of "mortality", then you will be aware of all that you have been and all that you are, all at once. This should be a strong incentive for living each day of your lives in harmony with yourselves and others, for once the blessing/curse of forgetfulness is lifted, you may not like what you see or remember. Yet you must accept it, if you are to move beyond your mistakes and return to the pure essence of what you were when you first came into being.

The Afterlife

I think one of the reasons people fear death so much is that they feel they can't be sure what happens next. We spend inordinate amounts of time worrying about the afterlife, about whether those who have passed on are all right, whether they're happy, or whether they even still have consciousness at all.

Unfortunately, many belief systems just contribute to the fear, to the extent that people spend much of their time trying to prevent death altogether instead of viewing it as a continuation of life, a moving forward to another phase of existence. What I have found, however, is that people who have come to embrace the concept that "dead" does not mean "no longer in existence" tend to be less worried about what happens after we die.

Naturally, I was glad to have the opportunity to talk about this with Niall, since the Sidhe were bound to have an interesting take on things, long-lived as they are.

Me: Beloved, can you clarify for me what happens after death? So many people grieve over their deceased loved ones and worry about whether that loved one is all right or even still exists.

Niall: *You have those now who study this, who seek more information on what happens to a human spirit after physical death. Many of those who communicate with spirit guides, angels, and others know that physical death is not the end of your existence. Your science even tells you that matter is not destroyed; it merely changes form. Thus, a human spirit is not harmed by death, no matter the method of parting the soul from the body.*

You know that there are some who refuse to admit or perceive that they are dead, and those are the ones who linger on as ghosts in the realms close to the third dimension. But at any time, even souls who linger may choose to pass on to the next phase of their existence. For humans, this often involves another descent into form, another lifetime, another lesson or set of lessons to learn. But never is death an end of existence.

Dying is not a true parting; it is only a passage from one state of being to another. Those who must part through this process will see each other again, and when you do not experience time as linear with its arbitrary divisions, you soon realize that this perceived separation does not last long. Those who remain behind in the earth plane, still wearing the vehicle of a physical body, must realize that it is only in their perception that any separation occurs at all. This may seem scant comfort to some, but once they realize that "dead" does not mean "gone," they may find themselves thinking of death in a different light.

Indeed, there are those who have been able to maintain contact with a loved one for a time after the loved one's death. Gradually, as minds and hearts open to what is possible, more and more people begin to perceive the spirits of their loved ones surrounding them, sometimes watching or guiding them from across the veil.

The very knowledge that death is not an end will open the door to perception for some people. While it is not healthy to hold onto a deceased loved one and prevent them from passing onward to their next lifetime and their next set of lessons when it is time for them to do so, there is also a comfort in knowing that you will reunite with that loved one again. Reunite is an inaccurate term, however, for how can you reunite with that from which you were never truly parted in the first place?

Groups of human souls tend to reincarnate together, lifetime after lifetime. A part of you will always be connected to a part of your loved ones, because separation is only illusion. Just remember that the descent into form and matter is only a very limited part of existence. There is so much more beyond the realm of the third dimension. Existence and the experience thereof is limitless. Consciousness is limitless. Love is limitless.

Therefore, the parting of a spirit from a temporary physical form cannot be an end in itself. It is merely a change in form. If you learn not to fear this change, you will no longer fear death. It is more like the removal of a worn garment, which may then be exchanged for a new one. But spirit, regardless of what form it happens to take or what garments it may be wearing, remains spirit, and the individuation of that spirit continues its existence armed with the knowledge gained from all of its experiences and forays into the third dimension and elsewhere.

Me: Is the place to which the Sidhe withdrew when they left this dimension the same as the place where human souls go when they die?

Niall: *Not exactly. The Otherworld, as you call it, has many different realms and pockets contained within it and adjoining to it. There are some places where these areas intersect, where you might occasionally see human souls intermingling with other types of beings. But for the most part, after their death, humans go to an area where they meet with loved ones, guides and advisors, and that process is overseen in a different manner altogether.*

There are some areas in the Otherworld where the environment is relatively static, and others where it is almost constantly changing, and this can prove distracting to spirits whose consciousnesses are not yet ready to acclimate to such conditions. The degree to which a being can adjust to an alternate reality varies depending on their individual vibration and the stage they are at in their soul's development. Different types of beings thrive in different environments even within a single dimension, just as in the earth realm, where you have land-based life, water-based life, and more.

Me: So, you indicated that there are other dimensions even beyond the Otherworld where beings can reside.

Niall: *Many. The universe is vast, and there are worlds within worlds. Consciousness itself is infinite, so why should the All That Is be any different? There are many other places and planes, many different beings. The Sidhe are certainly not the only denizens of the Otherworld, nor is the Otherworld the only place that can be reached.*

Me: Could you explain to me more about the concept of moving somewhere else after death? I have read various pieces of literature that talk about a spirit moving onward to somewhere else or to a different phase of one's journey. This would seem to indicate that a spirit does not always remain close to the third dimension or even continue to incarnate here after death.

Niall: *If you are thinking of the analogy of life as a classroom, then you will be familiar with the concept of institutions of higher learning. It would make no sense to repeat the same classes indefinitely once you had grasped the lessons inherent in those particular classes. So, too, do spirits progress.*

There are many "classrooms" to which spirits may go, and once a spirit has developed sufficiently to move onward to more expansive learning experiences, it is free to do so. Most human spirits incarnate on the earth plane repeatedly, as it can take many lifetimes to assimilate the most basic of lessons. But those who do so successfully may indeed move onward to other realms of being and other types of experiences.

Be aware that you have free will. This is why spirits who refuse to move on in their development are not forced to do so. They may be persuaded, but they may not be forced. You will never be forced to learn a lesson before you are ready. In like manner, you will not be forced to linger on in a class from which you have already graduated.

There is a way out of this wheel of incarnation, as humans experience it. It requires developing oneself spiritually to a point at which the lessons inherent in third-dimensional physicality are no longer needed, a point at which they have all been internalized and one is ready to move beyond the "101" level of classes and on to another level. Not all such lessons are learned in the third dimension, so this would involve a "moving on" to other places, other states of existence.

Me: Does this mean that once we are finished with the cycles of human incarnation, we must then part from our loved ones still engaged in those cycles?

Niall: *You are still thinking with a limited perception. At the higher levels of being, there is no sense of parting or loss. So no, you do not part from your loved ones at that stage, or at least, you do not perceive it as a parting. Instead, you perceive it as an enfolding, a much deeper level of connection to All That Is, which includes you, your loved ones, and all other individuations of spirit. Your connection to your loved ones endures throughout all of existence.*

Journal Entry, February 20, 2009

Today as I was waking up, I was thinking about the idea of having to grow old—which is daunting enough by itself—and then having to die. I was struck by how horrible it would be if I died and forgot everything that I currently know…if I ceased to be what I know as "myself". The following conversation with Niall ensued:

Me: Will you still think the same of me when this body ages and I'm grey and wrinkled?

Niall: *Of course. That form isn't you; it's only the body you're wearing for this lifetime.*

Me: I'm afraid that when I die, I'll get to the other side and you won't be there.

Niall: *I will be there, I assure you. You shouldn't worry about this.*

Me: I guess part of what I'm afraid of is that I'll never be this aware again. That I'll cross the veil and I won't still be me.

Niall: *You're afraid it will be vague and unformed, like a dream. That your thoughts won't be clear and you won't remember who you are.*

Me: Yes, exactly.

Niall: *Beloved, did you never consider that it might be your life there in the physical realm that is the dream, and your life here, the reality?*

Remember what I said to you before: every time you learn a lesson you needed to learn, every time you set aside another bit of your doubt and fear and open yourself to all that is truly possible, you become a little more like yourself. You are like a sleeper being awakened slowly, by degrees, and with each step of the process, more of the shell you have surrounded yourself with falls away.

In the past, much of your perception of who you were was like a mask, a made-up identity to help you relate to the world and yourself in it. Gradually, you need this façade less and less, and you begin to shed it the way a serpent sheds its skin. By the time you pass the veil, you will have recovered much of yourself, so that instead of losing yourself, you gain the remaining pieces of the puzzle, and so become whole.

That is the way it is supposed to work. Many people do not open themselves sufficiently to gain back all the pieces of their puzzles in one lifetime, and so must go back again to recover the lost bits. At least, this is how I perceive the process, having watched you for so many of your lifetimes.

The last comment was delivered with a gentle smile for me as I ruefully agreed that I must have been working on my issues for, as he'd indicated, "so many" lifetimes! It takes a while to learn some lessons, it seems, but at some point, light finally begins to dawn.

CHAPTER EIGHT

REFLECTIONS ON CONSCIOUSNESS

Free will and individuality vs. the concept of an egoless state of oneness with all of creation is a complex issue. Certainly, it has provided fodder for many a debate among spiritualists and religious leaders. This very issue is at the center of many of the challenges we face on this planet today.

One such challenge is the human tendency to get caught in what I call the 3-D trap. Living in these solid bodies with our free will and unique genetic compositions, the sensation and notion of being individual is almost overpowering. Unfortunately, this perception distances us from those around us—even those with whom we are in closest contact. We are fiercely protective of our "personal space," and the instinct for survival often overshadows everything else.

We sometimes get the idea that no one could possibly understand how we feel or how we think. If we find a person who can do just that, we feel extremely lucky or blessed. Often, our quest for a mate is for someone who will complete us, as we instinctively sense that we are missing something in our essential makeup. We are concerned mainly with our bodies, our ideas, our thoughts, our needs, goals and desires.

Think about it. When we seek out friends or mates, do we typically do it because we sense a need in the other person that we could fill, or do we tend to do it because we have a need that we want the other person to fill—because we're lonely, horny, or bored? On a daily basis, how often do most of us reach out to others in need, when there is no clear benefit to ourselves?

As a species, humans are capable of amazing generosity and truly selfless acts. Every time we see such a thing in action, it lifts our spirits and fires our admiration. But we are also guilty of selfish aggrandizement and gain at the expense of others. Unfortunately, this latter behavior is widely reinforced in the media, on reality television, in politics and big business practices. News of conflict and strife too often overshadows transcendent moments of connection, which become lost in the shuffle.

Many self-help books try to tell us how to better ourselves, how to strive for self-improvement, self-actualization, greater self-awareness. A few sources even tell us how to begin to relate to others and see ourselves as part of a much bigger picture, but often this is eclipsed by the need of ego to define itself more clearly. We spend a great portion of our lifetimes trying to figure out who we are as individuals.

It isn't so much that human beings are inherently selfish, but that we are too easily content with a micro-focus when what we need is a macro-focus. We automatically give our attention to those things we perceive as having direct and immediate impact on our lives and tend to ignore those we perceive as distant and unrelated to us. This type of spiritual nearsightedness can easily sabotage our development and leave us short of our ultimate goal. Distracted by our search for Self, we fail to see that if we could renew our connection to the whole of existence and see ego as secondary, we'd find the very completion and actualization we were searching for all along.

Unity and Individual Development

In pondering the above issues, I asked Niall about the concept of oneness vs. individuality. Since my question was non-specific, he answered first in a personal sense relating to the two of us, and then expanded the picture to a more general view.

He told me that in the sense that everything is part of everything else and all things are one thing, he and I are one. We also have individual consciousness, so we aren't the same being. But as I asked him and he confirmed, when we are speaking to each other, what I perceive as telepathy from him to me and vice versa, he perceives as the two of us partially merged, with the information from both of us circulated within the two-in-one of "us." Regarding our personal connection, he said:

You and I simply are, and have been together in this way for a long time. In the sense of the oneness you asked about, we are part of each other, both a part of "us." You must think of this state of unity as the safe place from which either of us may go forth and affect whatever it is we need to affect in the world. It is also the safe place to which we may return when our tasks are done or when we need comfort or support. You may return to me in this way at any time, and I will always be here.

So you see that you are never truly alone, never truly separate. This is what I meant when I told you, "There is no separation between me and thee." Know also that in another sense, neither of us ever really leaves the other, so it is only a part of your perception that needs to return, only a part of your perception that has ever been "away".

On a greater scale, the important thing for humans to realize is that the idea that they are separate from all other beings is illusion. The only separation occurs in their perception of themselves as completely autonomous individuals, via a construct that philosophers have termed the ego. While ego allows beings to develop at different rates and accomplish different tasks, it also contributes to the illusion that what one does will not affect anyone else. The reality is that there is no separation.

Think of separation as an imaginary partition that some beings erect between themselves and others. They do it for various reasons, and indeed individual consciousness has its purpose, even among the Sidhe. But the Sidhe are both aware of themselves as individuals and as part of the whole, both at the same time. There is never a time in which we believe ourselves entirely separate, as many humans do. Thus, what one of us does affects all, and we are instantly aware of the effects of our actions. We do not have either the benefit or the detriment inherent in the illusion of separateness as a state of being. You might say that separateness is not an illusion that will work on us. The more humans become aware of themselves as part of a much greater whole, the less they will be affected by this illusion.

Me: Is the oneness you speak of related to the concept of ascension?

Niall: *Yes, although it might be helpful to think of ascension not as a rising to some heaven or height, but more as a merging of your vibrations with the vibrations of other states of being. This is how one traverses the dimensions—by increasing or slowing one's vibratory state to align with those of the beings or dimensions you are trying to reach.*

We are aware that some think of ascension as an exalted state of enlightenment that removes one from more "earthbound" pursuits.

However, rather than the idea of learning how to leave all earthly considerations or attachments behind, perhaps a more useful concept would be the idea of learning how to form true connections with other beings and states of being, as well as connections with the Earth itself. In a sense, no matter what dimension we inhabit, we who have our being in the spirit of this planet are all Earthbound. Rather than seeking to escape it, one might instead seek to merge with it. One might then gain a different perspective as to what constitutes ascension or enlightenment.

Me: So are you saying that ascension and enlightenment are two different things?

Niall: *You are finding the semantics difficult to understand; my sympathies. I will try to clarify. When an entity begins to reincorporate the fragments of himself into a unified whole, the natural result is a change in his vibratory state. When the integration process is complete, it becomes possible for him to then change his physicality from a more solid 3-D form to a form you would call non-corporeal or higher-dimensional. This, then, is what you think of as physical ascension.*

A person who has sufficiently altered his vibrations can then manifest himself in any dimension or form he wishes. It is only because they have fragmented themselves and their energies to a detrimental level that most humans are not currently able to change their manifested physicality in this way. It would be fair to say that the process of self-integration and the attainment of wholeness—a state you would think of as "enlightened"—leads naturally to the ability to achieve physical ascension. Does this make more sense to you?

Me: Yes, that helps. Could you tell me what it's like to transition out of the third dimension?

Niall: *Ah, beloved, it is an experience of pure bliss. Your whole being becomes lighter and lighter until you are suffused with light. At the same* *time, emotion builds within the core of you until you feel that you will explode or perhaps implode—and that is much of what happens. Every particle of your body fills with light and you merge with it. You become aware that you have complete control over your atoms and molecules, and can change your composition at will. There is no pain with this change. It is more like an explosion of joy, or an expansion into peace, or whatever you make of it.*

Me: My next question relates to the limitations one experiences in a 3-D environment. It seems that various cultures have developed the idea that when one becomes enlightened, one need not return to the third dimension except perhaps to teach or guide others. This would imply that being in the third dimension means for most of us that we are somehow inferior, or at least not as advanced as we could be, and that when we do finally manage to become enlightened, we're out of here for good. Can you shed some light on this?

Niall: *With regard to the dimension in which a being currently resides—it is not so much a matter of perceived height or spiritual advancement, but rather a matter of speed at a molecular level. Is something that vibrates faster more enlightened or somehow better or superior to something that vibrates more slowly? Arguably, a stone vibrates at a much slower rate than a human, yet stones and crystals are ancient beings of great enlightenment.*

Lighter, denser, higher, lower, faster, slower—these are all labels you use to refer to your own vibration or to the physical state of a thing or being. When water is frozen, you call it ice, and when it is heated to the point of evaporation, you call it steam. But the molecules that form it remain the same; they have merely changed their state from one density to the other. None is inherently better. All that really changes from your perspective is the purpose to which you put the water in its various states. In one state, it returns to the atmosphere, in another, it quenches your thirst, and in yet another, it chills your drink or preserves your food. Which state is better depends on the need and the circumstance.

Enlightenment, or what we would call wholeness or integration, is more about an attitude and state of spirit in connection to the whole than about whether one has yet slipped out of the third dimension for the last time. We said before that enlightenment or self-integration leads naturally to physical ascension, the ability to change one's vibratory rate and traverse the dimensions at will. We did not say that everyone who resides in a different place than the third dimension is necessarily either ascended or enlightened.

Bear in mind all that we have said before; just because you are no longer in a body, it does not automatically follow that you are yet whole. You are, one hopes, in better touch with your own "higher consciousness," but even debriefed, disincarnate human spirits are often still very much damaged and in need of healing and integration, and a period of rest between transitions into another form. Learning and progress may still occur between lifetimes, but it depends on the events of the most previous lifetime and the condition of the spirit on leaving the third dimension.

Consider spirits of the dead who have not been able to move on in their development. They are currently of a different vibratory state and in a different dimension than beings who are still wearing a dense physical body, and yet they are stagnant, while many of those currently in 3-D bodies are hard at work bettering themselves and the world around them. It is important not to equate one's current dimension of residence with superiority or inferiority of spirit.

The Sidhe did not transition out of the third dimension because we found it to be inferior. We left because we wished to avoid further confrontation with humans. Try to envision the day when we can walk openly in the world beside humankind, all of us moving freely between the third dimension and those beyond. As we said before, this idea of inferiority and superiority must be set aside if true harmony is to occur.

It is not enough that humans merely learn to be aware of how their actions affect all things. Being aware of the consequences of one's actions and stopping first to consider how a given action will affect others is an important first step, but it is only a small part of a much larger change.

Me: So "enlightened" is more a state of living in oneness or deep harmony with all other beings than of living in one dimension or another?

Niall: *Again, we fall into semantics, but yes, that is the general idea. In order to be one with all things, you must truly know all things. In order to truly know a thing, you must merge in essence with that thing (or being), so that you know it on the deepest of levels. You, beloved, are learning how to do this with me. Every time our essence mingles, you are more aware of me and find yourself more able to pick up my communications to you, sense what I am feeling, and perceive things that relate to my very nature. The more practiced you become at this, the more you will be able to know what it is to "be" me. This is but a part of the depth of connection we have experienced and will experience. We are connected on the deeper levels, some of which you do not as yet remember in your current physical identity.*

Amergin spoke in his poetry of being many different creatures and things. In the same way, humans can gradually learn to know all things on the deep level that we have just mentioned. However, even if you merged your essence with a different being on a daily basis for the rest of your life, you would not have reached this state of harmony with all things in the space of one human lifetime.

Me: Have the Sidhe reached this state, and if so, does this constitute enlightenment?

REFLECTIONS ON CONSCIOUSNESS

Niall: *Remember that the Sidhe have been at this for a very long time. Then consider how many different beings have lived on this planet since life first emanated here. There are those whose physical, third-dimensional forms are now extinct, but whose spirits still exist, as well as all the beings still with you in your plane of experience.*

It may be that we fit your definition of enlightened, but this does not mean all-knowing. Nor are we perfect. An entity can be wise, ancient, and experienced in many states of being, and still have much to learn. We would hope that we can continue to learn and develop. Considering the division between human and Sidhe, we have not yet reached the level of harmony with all beings. Are we not seeking the remedy for this even as we speak?

Me: Yes, and I'm extremely glad of that. On a related but slightly different note, the concept of universal harmony and the idea of becoming one with all things—or at least trying to—brings up another question. Some people report that when they are shamanic journeying or out-of-body for whatever reason, or even temporarily displaced by another entity while full-body channeling, they sometimes feel that they lose their individual consciousness and have a hard time returning to it. Can you explain what is happening with these experiences?

Niall: *Yes. On rare occasions, a person becomes disoriented on a soul journey and finds it difficult to regain his sense of individuality. Even more rarely, a person becomes lost completely, and cannot find his way back to third-dimensional reality. We Sidhe, or "the faeries," have even been blamed on occasion for just such occurrences, when a human lost the sense of his individual consciousness or was altered by his experiences while journeying on a cosmic level. These altered or fragmented personalities were said to have been "away with the faeries" or "carried" by the faeries, and never quite the same when they returned. However, such blame is misapplied; these occurrences are generally not caused by the Sidhe.*

As we have just mentioned, sometimes people journey into alternate realities, lose themselves in the greater consciousness of the cosmos or in the perception of a reality they cannot make sense of, and cannot put their individualities back together again in order to return. Fortunately, this happens only rarely, and the more spiritually integrated an individual is before he begins his journey, the less likely he is to lose himself in infinity. By the time the serious seeker manages to experience more advanced soul journeys such as this, he is usually far better prepared for it. And if he feels himself becoming lost or disoriented, there is help—someone who will guide him back to his usual state of consciousness—if he calls for it.

Even those who have experienced these things on a deep level still have far to go in their understanding of the many different facets of reality. The determining factor is the ego structure and the ability of the individual to leave his current perception of himself behind—to accept a radical challenge to his paradigms, and yet still retain a sense of individuality to which he can return after he experiences such a revelation.

The eventual goal is to be of a dual nature, able to be at one with the cosmos but still able to summon one's individuality when needed. Our best advice in this matter is that humans first spend time gathering up the scattered bits of themselves and becoming whole. As you work toward wholeness, you can still get to know other beings on the deep levels we spoke of, and indeed, we encourage you to do this.

Me: Some of the ideas being presented by various sources now—such as the notion that there truly is no separation and that our reality is all just illusion—can be rather mind-blowing, and in some ways, even uncomfortable to contemplate.

Niall: *In order to understand why these things are difficult for some people to grasp, think on the nature of humans themselves. Humans, for all that they are agents of change, are remarkably resistant to change of any kind. It* *is a paradox of humanity that the Sidhe have yet to understand. Humans often strive toward the very thing that they resist with all their might, and the thing they fear is often also the thing they yearn for.*

People want to feel themselves part of the whole of the universe; they have an instinctive yearning for belonging, yet they are terrified of losing their personalities, their egos. They cling to the usual and familiar even when they know they must change. When this struggle is resolved, then the fragmented self will begin to heal and the spirit will no longer fear change and loss. When you are no longer fragmented, but whole, you will see that rather than losing yourselves, you have found yourselves instead. In a state of fully realized potential, there is no loss.

Me: So loss is another form of illusion? It is just another of the stories we tell ourselves?

Niall: *Yes. That being the case, why not tell stories of joy and abundance instead? You see this repeatedly in cases where people who have been adequately supported, nurtured and encouraged have gone on to achieve great things for themselves, precisely because they believed that they could do or be anything they wanted.*

Others, put down and told they were nothing, have often not reached their potentials. Instead, they chose to believe the negative, crippling opinions of others. It takes a great deal of strength to overcome this type of negative programming. Why? Because stories have power. Stories lead to beliefs, and beliefs inform and create everything you manifest in your life. In essence, you are what you believe. This is why words have such power, why names have such power.

One effect interacting with the Sidhe can have is that it can help us become much more aware of our place in the world, and of the responsibilities that come along with that awareness. The shift of paradigms and change in perspective can be quite significant. Niall was not jesting when he told me that maintaining a relationship with one of the Sidhe could literally turn one's world or perspectives upside down.

Perhaps one of the most important discoveries one can make is the awareness that as a part of the All That Is, our energy, actions and choices, however small they might seem, all contribute to the harmony or disharmony of the universe as a whole. All that we do matters.

Responsibility is not a particularly positive word to many people, because the very term implies that there is work involved. However, not all of that work has to be unpleasant. It may not be easy, and at times it may even seem quite challenging, but once the crucial step forward is made, taking responsibility for one's own state of being usually brings great relief and an increased sense of peace.

Just as it is important to learn to view ourselves with honesty and integrity, it is equally important to be patient, understanding and loving with ourselves. We all make mistakes along our paths. Mistakes, however uncomfortable they may feel at the time, are what help us grow and make us aware of cause and effect. They help us see beyond our momentary personal needs to a larger picture in a much longer span of existence that comprises more than just one human lifetime.

Regardless of where we are on our individual paths, we are on a journey of learning, along with countless others who are on similar journeys. Together, we are all constantly co-creating the immense symphony of the universe.

CHAPTER NINE

AWAKENING

All through my current lifetime, I'd been aware of small events and synchronicities that hinted there might be more to my existence than met the eye. Some were snippets of what seemed to be memories—so strong that they caused me much distress, as they did not seem to fit into the context or timeline of the life I'd been leading.

As in most cases, I kept finding ways to explain all the synchronicities away, or, in the case of the memories for which I could find no logical explanation, I simply relegated them to the back of my mind, burying them so that I would not have to continue puzzling or worrying over them. This went on for well over three decades.

One psychic reading in particular stands out for me, because at the time it was given, it struck me as rather incomprehensible. We'd just gotten into the session when the reader suddenly gave me a very direct look. "Are you ever afraid that you won't be able to get home?" she asked.

The question confused me. I had never had a moment's worry over my ability to safely drive from somewhere in my city back to my house, and for that matter, I'd never worried about getting back safely even when I was on a longer road trip. But I had gone to visit Ireland once, and as the plane had lifted from the tarmac to take me back to the United States, I'd felt inexplicably devastated by leaving—an emotion I'd had to hide from my fellow passengers so as not to upset anyone.

When the reader asked her question, I thought of that moment, and gave the only answer that occurred to me at the time—one that came from my soul. "Only where it concerns Ireland."

Tears came to my eyes as I spoke, and the reader stared at me. "Look at you," she said wonderingly, as it was obvious that somehow, she'd hit on something that my subconscious had known but my conscious mind had not.

That reading was one of the incidents that I filed away in a corner of my mind for future reference, because I had no other explanation for why I might feel worry about not getting home to Ireland, when Ireland had never been my home in this lifetime. "A past life, perhaps," I reasoned, and left it at that. The real explanation for that part of the reading didn't become clear to me until much later—about fifteen years later, in fact.

Sidhe Soul in a Human Body

By the time of my reconnection with Niall in 2008, many small synchronous events, random comments by various unconnected people, readings, and things sensed by intuitives and healers all had combined to add up to one huge question—whether I had, in fact, once been one of the Sidhe.

Looking back through my journals leading up to the day of my Awakening when I finally acknowledged this very basic facet of my existence, I could see how many times I'd almost reached that state of acceptance. The question had arisen again and again, and each time I'd forced it down, not wanting to make assumptions. But regardless, the question still kept rising to the surface, until finally I could not continue setting it aside or refusing to acknowledge it.

With that acknowledgment came a certain amount of fear, because there was still a large part of me that was afraid to allow myself to believe a thing that seemed so far-fetched. I feared the opinion of others and was realistic enough to know that there were many who would never believe that I could be a Sidhe soul in a human body, not to mention those who would openly offer censure or even derision. But my delaying and ignoring of my personal truth made it no less important, no less true, and finally, there was nothing left to do but embrace what my spirit had been trying to tell me all along. I knew it was only fear and doubt that made me delay so long in admitting the truth to myself, but finally, the time had come to cast aside these limitations.

Once I'd realized that my soul's origin was Sidhe and that I did indeed have another home somewhere else, and that home was presently beyond my reach, then the meaning of the reader's question from over fifteen years prior came to me with complete clarity. Was I ever afraid that I wouldn't be able to get home?

When "home" meant the Otherworld and the world of the Sidhe, the question suddenly made perfect sense. I was, indeed, trying to do whatever it took to get myself back home to my Sidhe family, and at the time of that reading, there must have been some part of my subconscious, as yet un-awakened, that was worried this might not happen.

Naturally, the Awakening occasioned a lot more conversation between Niall and myself. When I began to question him about how it could have come about that I, as Sidhe, came to be walking around wearing a human body and experiencing reincarnation, I suddenly got the sense that it had been because of a mission I'd undertaken—one intended to help gather information about what it meant to be human. Considering the problems that humans and Sidhe had with one another in the past, it made sense that somehow, we'd try to find a way to bridge the gap.

In pondering the way the Morrigan had reached out to me, helping to Awaken me to who and what I was, more pieces of my Sidhe memory began to resurface. One of the memories I had recalled earlier but not been able to explain—a vision of myself being initiated into a group of black-clad female warriors—now became clear to me. I realized that as one of the Morrigan's Badbha Catha, or "crows of battle," I'd been sent here into this human existence by her request—not to wage war, but to bring back knowledge gained by a firsthand experience of humanity.

This awareness resonated deeply within me, as did the realization that I'd had to leave loved ones behind in the Otherworld in order to do it—loved ones who were nonetheless all around me, merely hidden from my perception until I reached the stage where I was able to Awaken and remember myself again.

As I began to wrap my mind around the knowledge that I had a detailed history, a life and existence in the Otherworld that included an entire Sidhe family, I needed Niall's insight more than ever to help me begin to understand the circumstances in which I now found myself. I was beginning a recovery from spiritual amnesia, and I had no instruction manual or map for such a journey. At that point, a rather astonishing conversation ensued:

Niall: *Hiding has become a policy with us for so long that it will be difficult to convince all that the time for such is passing. This is a situation that requires much delicacy and preparation. Hence, your incarnation into a human body. As you have surmised, the easiest way to walk among humans was to send some of us to join their ranks and go through what they experience. Many of your fellow Badbha went on such reconnaissance. Many never returned. After the first few, we realized that each would need another on this side to guide and guard them, to help bring them back to themselves. But by then it was too late for some.*

In the future, however, once more humans begin to work toward wholeness, many of those Sidhe souls who became lost in the human incarnation cycle and forgot themselves will Awaken through this process.

Me: Was there anything you wanted to say to me concerning my Awakening and what's been happening between my lifetimes?

Niall: *These are separate topics, love. (Pause, during which I wondered if we'd temporarily lost the connection, and started reaching for him.) Yes, I'm here; don't worry. I am thinking how best to respond. You want to know why it took you so long to realize you were Sidhe, and why we did not simply tell you outright.*

Even if I had told you, you would not have believed me at first. You had become so damaged by low self-esteem and the belief that you were less than worthy, that had I told you that you were Sidhe, you would not have allowed yourself to believe me. I dropped hints. For the entirety of your current lifetime, I dropped hints, which you now recognize as what they were.

You had to bring yourself to ask the question, love. And your spirit guides had to answer. They are working with us toward better understanding between our peoples, and they have been of great help in bridging the gap. They treat you no differently than they treat any of their purely human charges. Many things will change now that you have begun to Awaken.

The guides will continue to help you, but you must look even further within for some of your answers. You may have to consider a regression to recover some of your lost memories. I cannot recover all of them for you. We cannot circumvent the process you are undergoing. But we are close, now. Closer than ever before. It may be that when you leave there this time, you can come home to stay.

Me: Now that I know why we are connected and realize where I truly come from, there is a certain level of panic and loss that has eased in me. I'm still dealing with the revelation, but deep down I always knew. I was just so afraid I'd be wrong. I did not want to be presumptuous.

Niall: *Humility is a double-edged sword. Ask.*

Me: What can you tell me about us, now that I at least know what I am?

Niall: *I wondered when you would ask this. Our union, beloved, is of long and ancient duration; you are to me the mirror of my own spirit. I told you before that we are a match. Why else do you think one of the first things I communicated to you was love poetry? We are, my love. You feel it now, don't you? Hold that knowledge to you; hold me to you. Have no fear.*

I cannot tell you much more. It is for you to remember, at least in part. There are things I may share with you, but for now, perhaps it is best if you just let yourself feel. From feeling comes knowledge, and surety, and resonance.

I am so glad this has happened. This will make things so much easier. Do you see now why you must not think of yourself as less? This little revelation will have significantly leveled the playing field. But I will hold you to a higher standard, now. I will be stern with you if you begin to think of yourself as inferior. You will be challenged to grow faster, to uncover layers of memory, but I will always be here to help you.

Journal Entry, May 27, 2011 – A Symbolic Dream

I dreamed that I was in a forested area with a small clearing, at the edge of which was built a circular stone dais. Atop the dais at the back of the circle were some tall standing stones—no more than five, I think. Two were toward the extreme left and right of the dais, standing at a slight angle to the others, and three were grouped close together, sides touching, forming a wall. In front of this wall, built into the floor of the dais, was a small pool of water. Three low steps at the front of the dais led up to the pool of water.

As I approached it, I saw what I thought were a pair of small forest animals scurrying away farther into the woods, carrying/dragging along with them a circular object that looked like a crown made of antlers. The feeling was that of preparation, as though something was going on farther in, and the forest denizens were getting ready for something.

I went up onto the dais and knelt to look into the pool, and for just an instant, it was as though the level of the water lowered so that I could see into it more clearly. Lying at the bottom of the pool was a gold crown. It seemed to be encircled by tiny golden stylized images of women's heads, most of the faces showing only the most basic of features, (eyes, noses, mouths) but without specific identifying details to make each one unique. They looked a lot like theater masks.

When I saw them, it occurred to me that they possibly represented facets of me that were as yet unknown to me—all my experiences in total, including my human past lives. They stood in a ring around the crown, as if they guarded it. One spot at the front only held a partial face—this lifetime, not yet finished? Next to that was one empty spot with no face/mask. My Sidhe life that was interrupted, or maybe the rest of my journey of existence? A part of me as yet unformed?

All I knew as I stared at the crown was that I had to reclaim it, and if I did so, it would mean reclaiming all those faces, all those parts of me that weren't known to me any longer. It occurred to me that I was bound not to like some of it. Some of those generic masks no doubt hid parts of me that I wouldn't like, but that I'd have to own anyway. I also knew that I could choose to step away from the pool, but if I did, I'd be leaving all those parts of myself behind.

For me, there was no question of what my choice would be. I looked at all those faces—all those masks—and forgave myself in advance for whatever was behind them. They were all parts of me; I'd have to own them no matter what they hid, no matter what mistakes or failings I found behind them.

I also knew that in order to reclaim the crown, whatever that symbolized, I'd have to immerse my face in the water. Even as I looked, I could see an image of a woman's face, like a dim reflection in the water that I couldn't quite see clearly. There was to be no reaching into the pool with a hand and pulling the crown out. Even as I realized this, the water level rose again, with the crown resting down on the bottom. If I wanted it, I'd have to plunge into the pool, face first. I somehow knew it was the only way.

I reached out one finger and gently touched the surface of the water, and it felt as though the air around me rang like a bell. Then I woke.

Living the Paradigm

The more time that went by after I was able to embrace the perception of myself as a Sidhe soul having a human experience, the more things fell into place in my daily life. Even when events were stressful, I found I was living each day with a groundedness, a deeper sense of peace and belonging than I'd ever experienced before in this lifetime.

I have been fortunate to find myself surrounded by human friends and family who view my Sidhe origins and associations as both believable and acceptable. Many of them have even sensed the energies of Sidhe around me or heard the occasional mental comment, and none of them are particularly surprised now if I sometimes happen to laugh or speak aloud in reply to someone on the other side of the veil. For that acceptance and love, I am deeply grateful.

In the years that have passed since the self-realization that we call Awakening, the lessons from my beloved family and friends in the Otherworld have been ongoing. There have been moments of profound realization and sheer delight, and also moments of doubt and struggle. Along with all of those moments, however, there is an underlying sense of joy and belonging that infuses and transforms everything I do, and makes me look at the world in a much different light. Perhaps the most wondrous thing of all is the knowledge and surety of who I am and what I am doing here, and knowing that the path I now travel is the right one for me.

Memories from my Sidhe life seem to come back to me in bits and pieces and flashes of insight, but the memories I have been able to recover make sense of so many things from my current human life that they provide further confirmation in and of themselves. It has indeed been as Niall said, like pieces of a puzzle being put back into place.

I have found that oftentimes, just as soon as I learn a lesson or something "clicks" for me, then the opportunity to use that rediscovered knowledge to help someone else soon comes into play, reinforcing the life lessons I've been given. Being able to share the knowledge I've gained the hard way is humbling—an honor and a blessing. I've made mistakes along the way, but I've also experienced successes, and I am grateful for both, because I've learned so much from both.

Some of the challenges I face seem daunting at times, and sometimes I need to repeat certain life lessons a few times before they fully sink in, but Niall and other members of my Sidhe family are always "just a thought away," as they put it, to offer guidance, healing or support if I need it. Their profound wisdom never fails to amaze and delight me.

I can no longer conceive of a life without the Sidhe in it. They are my past, my present, and my future. I am humbled and grateful beyond measure for their generosity and loving care in helping me make this transition back to myself.

I honor every person who has contributed to the growth and learning I have experienced since losing myself and now finding myself once again. It is my hope that each and every one of the many beautiful souls I've met here in the earth plane will find the path back to their pure, authentic selves.

To those who are steadfastly seeking their own paths of Spirit and the truth of their own Being-ness, I ask you to please never give up. Never let doubt or fear keep you from becoming all that you can be, or from being all that you are. You are, every one of you, vastly beautiful and wondrous. Walking among you, living with you, and learning from you has been and continues to be a privilege.

AFTERWARD

There was once a time when openly admitting that one felt oneself to have spiritual origins that were other than human would have been akin to sparking off a witch hunt. It would have been to place oneself under unwanted scrutiny and even ridicule. Nowadays, those sorts of stigmas are changing, and people are feeling gradually more able to safely be themselves, whoever or whatever that might be, though this is certainly not the case everywhere as yet.

As more eyes, minds and hearts open, our society as a whole moves slowly but surely toward a time and state where the norm could be acceptance, rather than the exclusion and rejection that has often characterized the past. My hope for any who have ever felt themselves to be *other* in some way is that along with their acceptance of themselves, they will also find support, love, and belief within the human community of which they are a vital and important part.

I asked Niall for any last comments he might have, especially with regards to healing for everyone, no matter their plane of residence or their current state of existence. But especially, I wanted to hear what he might say to all those who reside here in the physical realm, with all of its hustle and bustle, and all of its beauties and challenges.

I can think of no better way to wrap up a book of life lessons from the Sidhe than with the words that came though from my beloved:

No matter what a person's origins may be, human, Sidhe, or otherwise, Awakening is a process that everyone can experience, because in essence, Awakening is simply a reconnection to source, to the All That Is. Ultimately, the origin of all beings is Spirit itself. Awakening is the process of healing and reintegrating all the parts and facets of one's deepest self, rediscovering one's place in the cosmos, and recognizing one's true resonance. Allowing this process to unfold even in the face of doubt and uncertainty is one of the greatest challenges that all beings face.

The knowledge of your deepest self is within you always. All you need do is open to that wellspring, allow gratitude for all that you are to suffuse your being, and a world of wonder will open up to you. Each day can be lived as the gift and lesson that it is. All is potential, and the ability to make that potential become manifest is within each and every one of us. We wish you all blessings on this journey.

www.ingramcontent.com/pod-product-compliance
Lightning Source LLC
Chambersburg PA
CBHW071909290426
44110CB00013B/1339